UNIFIED POWER ®

UNIFIED POWER ®

CHARLES R. HOBBS
AND GREG W. ALLISON

UNIFIED POWER ENDORSEMENTS

"Charles R. Hobbs and Greg W. Allison have not only masterfully identified the key elements of institutional and personal integrity, but have done so with wonderful clarity. They have a gift for synthesizing timeless yet ever new principles of successful men and women and illuminating them with effective examples and powerful parables. Charles Hobbs long ago taught us how to think about and "improve" time. In this new "guide to the perplexed," he now with Greg Allison, teaches us how to think about and improve ourselves and our organizations. At a time when much of the public has lost confidence in many of the key institutions and leaders of our society, Unified Power is a clarion call for re-establishing what used to be called fundamental virtues as the foundations for individual and organizational power."

> —*Robert S. Wood,* Dean Emeritus, Center for Naval Warfare Studies, and Chester W. Nimitz Chair of National Security and Foreign Policy, U. S. Naval War College, former Director of Strategic Studies for the Chief of Naval Operations and consultant to the White House, Department of State, and the Department of Defense.

"Once again Dr. Charles Hobbs, with Greg Allison, gives meaningful insights about aligning our behavior with our beliefs. Unified Power comes as we allow core principles to govern our decisions and priorities. We would be wise to read and consistently review their superstructure model. Unified Power will ignite improvement in our performance and bring us peace and satisfaction in all our work."

> —*Craig Hanson,* President/Market Manager
> Simmons Media Group

"Charles Hobbs is one of the finest educators I have ever known. This exciting new book backed by his lifetime of experience and sprinkled with the wisdom of Greg Allison is a must read for everyone wanting to achieve maximum performance."

> —*Brent D. Peterson, Ph.D.*
> Chair, The Work Itself Group

Contents

Preface

We live in a world marked by great dichotomy. The demand for greater performance and increased productivity are relentless in our businesses and our personal lives. In the midst of these demands for more, scarcely a day goes by that we don't read or hear of another scandal, breech of ethics, or lapse of moral judgment. Our appetite for progress is so insatiable that our very society teeters on the brink of temporal, moral and spiritual bankruptcy under its pressure. Personal and corporate integrity and ethics have given way to relativism and greed. Time-honored standards of virtue are regularly abandoned in favor of expediency and a narcissistic sense of entitlement. The sheer magnitude and frequency of collapse in every aspect of society have increased to alarming levels more than anytime in our history.

Far too many people, especially those in Western society, have become too preoccupied with succeeding at any cost, winning through exploitation and intimidation, and pursuing short-term frills and thrills, rather than seeking long-term substance and meaning.

One need look no further for examples of these trends in recent years than to the many individuals and institutions, once considered and revered as enduring and above reproach, that now lay in ruins as a result of irreparable consequences growing out of unprincipled decisions and actions. Yet in almost every case, if decision-making and performance—whether on the individual or corporate level—had been grounded in principles of truth that have stood the test of time, literally millions of lives could have been spared pain, embarrassment, or ruin. We are left to ask: How and when did such core principles like integrity, faith, love and humility become so unpopular or so untenable that they would be discarded so easily and readily?

That said, we realize there are no large crowds standing in line to buy books or attend seminars that call for a return to a more Puritan work ethic, or to the principles of America's founding fathers, or even the moral values of previous generations we occasionally reflect on with nostalgia. But our collective unwillingness to incorporate such ethics, principles, and values in our lives certainly does not negate their vital role in the hearts and minds and actions of mankind. Nor does society's seeming lack of interest in such values negate the vital role they play in helping us attain the levels of performance expected of others—and that we expect of ourselves!

Unified Power represents a unique combination of the old and the new. Its foundational principles are grounded in philosophies, belief systems, and even architectural approaches that are as old as civilization, while the application of these principles to our current time grows out of modern organizational and behavioral science. The outcome for those who read and apply this book will be both a mindset and a value system that will increase your personal productivity while providing you with a more balanced and fulfilling lifestyle and personal philosophy. There can also be a far reaching outcome in empowering your organization with unification and quality productivity.

The early ideas for *Unified Power* came to Charles Hobbs as he was pursuing his doctorate in Learning and Teaching Theory at Columbia University under some of the most brilliant minds in his field of study. It was there that Charles became convinced that lives could be changed, not for just a few days, weeks, or months, but for a lifetime, if people were given the right training and tools. That germ of an idea ultimately took root and grew into the *Time Power System*—the very first time-management training program of its kind, which was taught for many years by Charles and his associates throughout the United States and in foreign countries, and which gave rise—sometimes directly and sometimes indirectly—to numerous other programs that were largely based on the principles Charles developed. In addition, Charles wrote the best-selling book, *Time Power*, which was named as one of the top 20 time-tested business management books by the editors of *Executive Book Summaries*.

Not long after the *Time Power System* was developed, Charles began formulating the groundwork for this book, *Unified Power*. In developing the concept of self-unification, he reasoned that there are foundational principles or truths that help bring balance, harmony, and appropriateness to a person's life, even as they enhance productivity. These principles derive not only from Charles's rigorous scholarly research but also from years of watching them both applied and abused in countless individual and business situations.

Greg Allison has made a significant contribution in providing content and context for the *Unified Power System* in today's world.

Taking the concept of self-unification to a much more powerful level, he has organized and brought enhancement to the principles Charles identified into the *superstructure model* as a personal framework and guide for empowering companies and individuals. He also provides significant insights and examples gleaned from years of leadership experience in corporate America.

The foundational principles we discuss in this book are not unique to us. Each has a historical basis that spans millennia and is found in virtually every enduring religious and time-tested secular cannon comprising principles of truth. What *is* unique about this book is how it will help you identify, apply, and become empowered with truths that sustain high self-esteem and produce optimal productivity at home and in the workplace.

Even with all the daily headlines of greed, corruption, and lapses in values, our combined experience has convinced us that there are still countless wonderful people and organizations that are living good lives and doing good things, which gives great cause for hope and optimism. Mankind's capacity to advance on principled conviction has not been lost; it's just dramatically veered off course in far too many cases. This book is about getting people, and, by extension, organizations and even societies, back on the right course of principle-centered thought and action.

The *Unified Power System* presented in this book not only provides a cogent answer for what your guiding principles should be, but also provides you, the reader, with practical tools to implement these principles in your planning and performance. Our intent in writing this book is to engender such a compelling impetus for change and force for good in your life and career that you will wonder how you ever got by without truly understanding, applying, and integrating the principles found herein. Your own personal superstructure awaits you in the pages that follow.

Charles R. Hobbs
Greg W. Allison

Introduction

How often do you have the kind of day when you feel you are on top of the world—when all the things you need to do are somehow done by day's end, when there is a tangible sense of harmony and congruity in all your dealings and interactions, and when events of the day just seem to go your way? Whether your time on such days is spent at work, with your family, or pursuing your favorite pastime, that feeling of being in control and of good things falling into place is one most of us yearn to experience more often.

Such days, of course, don't come entirely by chance or very often. They are the result of the many choices we make, both big and small, and how well we execute them. As we begin to consider how to secure better, more productive and fulfilling days, rather than those that seem to endlessly spin out of control we need to understand the difference between events we can control and events we cannot control. There are three realities each of us must face:

1. There are events you should control but you don't.
2. There are events you think you can control but you can't.
3. There are events you think you cannot control but you can.

There is absolutely no way you will ever be able to control every person, event or outcome in your life. (Those who think they can go nuts, or at the very least, drive those around them nuts.) There are circumstances we face that are not of our making; there are changes we encounter that are inevitable—and that often happen at speeds beyond our comprehension. But there are two facts you must never overlook: First, you always have choices; and, second, you can learn to control a far greater portion of what goes on around you than you think.

Sometimes it may seem that you're being buffeted by circumstances beyond your control. The source may be a co-worker who doesn't deliver, or a boss who won't listen to reason, or a child you know is headed for a fall. Or it could be someone who has run a stop sign and crashed into you, making you late for an appointment you can't be late for. We could provide you with an endless string of examples, but in almost every case you can make choices that will lead to maintaining control of a greater number of events in *your* life through practice and planning.

Regardless of the circumstances you face—and regardless of their origins—you will find yourself with far greater control and congruity as you use *Unified Power* to create a personal superstructure. Although the concept of a superstructure will be developed more fully in subsequent chapters, in its simplest form a superstructure is anything that is built on top of something else, either conceptually or physically, that in turn creates a foundation of lasting power.

When you base your life, relationships or career—and your choices—on a sure foundation of principles that have stood the test of time and that are secured by a strong framework of personal and organizational concepts, you will be far more likely to achieve greater success in all aspects of your life.

One immediate and significant benefit of taking charge of events in your life is the prized possession of high self-esteem. When you learn to control more of what happens around you, your self-esteem will increase, and with it you will see a marked increase in your personal productivity. As you learn to visualize yourself in a holistic, total life perspective, *Unified Power* will help you achieve definable, actionable, and demonstrable performance that has the power to change your life forever.

This book does not extol what some have called "profitable virtue" (doing the "right thing" for the sole purpose of deriving some tangible benefit), nor does it advocate one system of belief, ethic or morality over another. Rather, it maintains that there are certain enduring principles that have led all truly great achievers to greater accomplishment and fulfillment.

Some cynics may argue that there is sparse empirical data or no direct ROI correlation to measure the impact that such principles have on performance. While it may be difficult to quantify with certitude the net monetary effect such principles have on self-esteem and productivity, we have all seen the adverse effects on individuals, families and institutions when such core principles are abandoned or ignored in society. One need only scan the news on any given day for stories chronicling the devastating effects on personal lives, homes, and organizations when fundamental principles of truth have been discarded or forgotten.

The central premise of this book is that many of the personal, institutional, and societal problems seen today stem from the violation of certain intrinsic principles of truth that have existed throughout the ages. Our unwillingness or inability to adhere to such core principles has taken a serious toll on our collective and individual self-esteem and productivity. Incongruity, or the inability to align what should be valued most with actual performance, has been the result. In our view, this incongruity derives from:

A Lack of Integrity: Failing to make and keep commitments, dishonesty, deception, shading the facts, greed, opportunism, and taking undeserved credit.

A Lack of Faith: Living with doubt and fear, pessimism, cynicism, a distrust of others and self, and unwillingness to forgive others and ourselves.

A Lack of Love: Showing indifference or insensitivity to the feelings and needs of others, exhibiting selfishness, jealousy, and disrespect, making false judgments, and not striving for understanding.

A Lack of Humility: Being arrogant, prideful, easily angered, self-centered, pompous, insubordinate, self-adulating, and condescending.

However, we believe there is still much to be hopeful and optimistic about in the foundation of the superstructure we will help you build. This superstructure, *your* superstructure, will derive much of its strength and stability from four foundational cornerstones called the **Unified Power Principles: Integrity, Faith, Love, and Humility**.

In offering these four principles as the cornerstones of the superstructure foundation, we do not mean to suggest that they are all-inclusive. You will likely have other values that will add form and function to your superstructure, along with the four Unified Power Principles. This book will help you discover what these other unifying principles, or values, are and how they interconnect with the Unified Power Principles to add power and longevity to your superstructure framework.

Unified Power also includes three conceptual devices vital to the stability and effectiveness of any superstructure framework. These are **Congruity, Competency Plus,** and **Concentration of Power** (otherwise called **The Unified Power Cs**). Each of these plays a significant role in integrating the Unified Power Principles throughout your superstructure. By understanding how these three devices combine to create *Unified Power,* you will begin to experience greater control and congruity in your decision-making and actions, and you will capture far more often that feeling of life flowing in the way you imagine and intend.

As you consider the potential of *Unified Power* in your life or organization, ask yourself how much of your time is spent on actions you would consider of high value or that result in meaningful productivity. The truth is that most of us waste hours each day tinkering with tantalizing trivialities, sorting through the thick of thin matters, and dealing with a myriad of unproductive activities. The principles developed in *Unified Power* are designed to help you:

1. Take more effective control of events in your life.
2. Increase your ability to selectively identify, define, and accomplish your highest priorities in accordance with what you value most.
3. Become empowered with higher self-esteem and confidence.
4. Produce more consistent optimal results in your personal life and career.
5. Help to enhance quality productivity in the company and other organizations where you serve.

These are lofty, even ambitious, outcomes. To some, they may seem out of reach. But our experience in teaching and then watching individuals and organizations apply the principles that bring about these results has proven repeatedly the power that grows out of applying these principles. Consider the following example, which comes from one of Charles's experiences teaching the Unified Power Principles:

I was invited to teach my two-day seminar to twenty-one employees in a prospering distribution company in Detroit. Before I agreed to teach the seminar, I set the following ground rules with the company's human resource director.

- *Class participants had to agree to schedule at least five hours of uninterrupted personal planning time the day after the seminar to carry out the assignments I would give them.*
- *Knowing that when goals are properly written and executed life-changing results in optimizing a more productive life could well be the result, I specified that class members needed to take careful notes so they would be prepared to write their productivity goals at the end of the seminar.*
- *The participants needed to all agree to attend a one-day follow-up session six weeks after the seminar to give a progress report and receive follow-up instruction.*

I started the class by having participants stand, introduce themselves, and briefly explain their work assignments in the company. The third person to stand was Martha, who said she was secretary to a department manager and had been with the company two years. There was something about her professionalism that caught my attention when she spoke. After the introductions, we proceeded with the training.

As planned, I returned six weeks later to follow up on the assignments I had given the class throughout the seminar. All but three participants attended the follow-up, and all of them had written their unifying principles. All but two had completed writing and prioritizing their personal life goals and goals with the company. And they all reported spending productive time in writing their productivity goals.

But Martha had clearly gone above and beyond her assignment. She reported spending most of the day after the seminar in solitude planning, integrating what she had learned into her plan of action. She added, "Without exception, every morning since the class, I have been up at 5:30 a.m., instead of the usual 6:00 a.m. During this solitude planning time, I followed the guidelines you taught us in writing our productivity goals."

At the end of the follow-up session Martha requested a private interview with me to receive feed-back on her time management goals, which included written unifying principles, personal life goals, and goals with the company.

When I saw her number-one goal with the company I was amazed, perhaps even a little incredulous. This department secretary, who was near the bottom of the corporate ladder, had written, "Within three years I will be president of our company." As I began to question she interrupted by quoting, with a smile on her face, a thought I had shared with the class in the seminar just a few weeks earlier:

I have my direction. I will not hesitate. I will not deviate. I will not capitulate. And I will prevail.

I responded by saying, "Martha, it appears to me that you are setting about to take control of an anticipated event that others would say can't be done. I wish you the very best in what I'm sure you know will be a challenging undertaking." I then flew home, wondering what would become of this remarkable woman.

Martha's goal was ambitious, to say the least. Some might have even deemed it unrealistic and therefore self-defeating, given her relative lack of experience and the myriad of circumstances and machinations over which she would have little if any control. Often, trainers and consultants lose contact with those they've worked with, but in this case Charles crossed paths with Martha some years later. In like manner, we will return to Martha's ultimate experience with the Unified Power Principles later in the book.

Throughout this book, we will set forth a series of principles and courses of action that will challenge you, in some cases well beyond your level of comfort. In doing so we recognize that every day we all, to some extent, engage in unproductive, even counter-productive activities, whether at work or at home. But our years of experience working in and consulting for all kinds of organizations has reinforced a simple truth that most of us know instinctively but often fail to follow: When performance is not aligned with what we should be valuing most, productivity suffers first, followed almost immediately by a decline in self-esteem.

When implemented consistently through committed effort, *Unified Power* will help you take control of your life in ways you never before thought possible. As you develop and apply the principles and tools explored in this book, you will enhance your quality of life and increase your productivity in ways that will bring balance, harmony, and appropriateness in every aspect of your life. Doing so will require considerable effort. But as you begin to see and experience the outcomes, large or small, you will know with certainty that they were well worth the time and effort.

CHAPTER 1

The Superstructure:
Build with the End in Mind

*"Man alone can change his own pattern. Man alone is
the architect of his destiny. The greatest discovery in our
generation is that human beings, by changing the inner
attitudes of their minds, can change the outer aspects of their
lives."*

— *William Blake*

Imagine for a moment all the types of structures that exist today. A short list might include skyscrapers, mansions, tee-pees, barns, bridges, roller coasters, statues, and monuments. Some are made of steel, others of glass, wood, brick, or concrete. Now ask yourself what is it about these structures that make them unique. Are they more form than function? How were they constructed? What purposes do they serve? Are they intended to be temporary or permanent?

Next, think of some of the architectural and structural wonders that exist in the world today: the Taj Mahal, the Eifel Tower, the Statue of Liberty, the Sistine Chapel, the *U.S.S. Nimitz*, the space shuttle, and so on. If you were to choose your favorite, which would it be and why? Perhaps it's the engineering mastery, aesthetic beauty, or purpose and utility of the structure that draws you to it.

Upon hearing the term *superstructure*, many immediately think of modern marvels or magnificent ancient wonders. In our modern times, we might think of the Empire State Building, Hoover Dam, or the Golden Gate Bridge. Among ancient structures, the pyramids at Giza in Egypt or the Parthenon in Greece come to mind. Both were incredible superstructures of their time.

Consider the Greek Parthenon. Completed in 438 B.C. and dedicated to the Greek goddess of wisdom, Athena, the Parthenon has been acclaimed through the ages for its architectural integrity. Resting on a foundation of limestone atop the Athenian Acropolis, this superstructure is supported by a muscular framework of majestic Doric colonnades or pillars.

The Parthenon has been characterized by some experts as having an unbroken state of unified wholeness with near perfect balance and dimension. It is a masterpiece of form and function, qualifying it as one of the greatest architectural superstructures in the history of mankind.

But the term *superstructure* is not reserved just for the world of architecture.

A *superstructure* is any extension of an idea or entity that is formulated, developed, extended, or built atop a foundation of enduring form, function, and principle.

Coming from the Latin *super* (for *above*, or *in addition*) and *structure* (also from Latin and meaning *to build* or *to heap up*), the lexicon of *superstructure* permeates mathematics, science, engineering, technology, medicine, and numerous other sciences and disciplines. It is used to articulate structure, equation, and concept in everything from shipbuilding to dentistry. There is even an athletic shoe named the "Superstructure." This book could rightfully be considered a superstructure—created within a framework of ideas based on solid concepts of proven principles.

Be it a skyscraper, the bridge of a ship, a new car's electronic system, or a business plan, superstructures impact our lives in aesthetic or practical ways every day. For the purposes of this book, we want you to consider a superstructure as any individual or organization that has a foundation based on a core set of principles (or truths) that have stood the test of time and that also demonstrates a higher level of performance consistent with those principles.

The great writer C. S. Lewis classically illustrated the essence of a superstructure when he wrote:

> *Imagine yourself as a living house. God comes in to rebuild that house. At first, perhaps, you can understand what He is doing. He is getting the drains right and stopping the leaks in the roof and so on; you knew those jobs needed doing and so you are not surprised. But presently He starts knocking the house about in a way that hurts abominably and does not seem to make sense. What on earth is He up to? The explanation is that He is building quite a different house from the one you thought of — throwing out a new wing here, putting on an extra floor there, running up towers, making courtyards. You thought you were going to be made into a decent little cottage, but He is building a palace.* (Mere Christianity, 1952. Essays based upon radio addresses of 1941-1944.)

Before you can begin to build any sort of superstructure—whether it is a house, a business, a plan of action, a revolutionary new product, or a life fueled by meaning—a strong foundation must first be laid.

The intent of your structure must also be based on fundamentally sound principles in order to support and accomplish your intended purposes.

While considering material superstructures may increase our understanding of the concept, your personal superstructure is obviously not just a physical or material model but rather a reality of enduring form and meaningful function. As individual or collective as it may be, the standard blueprint of a superstructure must:

- Be based on solid and applied concepts
- Be built on time-tested, proven principles
- Maintain consistency in form and function throughout
- Be easily identifiable
- Provide intrinsic purpose and benefit
- Satisfy a vital need
- Support all other elements
- Provide a platform or framework for future growth

Given that many of our economic, political, and societal values are in a continuous state of flux—where markets and influences sway back and forth in winds that shift direction without warning; where the boundaries between right and wrong, good and evil, or ethical and improper are blurred and blend at every turn—there is a greater need today than ever before for enduring superstructures built on rock-solid principles. That these be anchored in accepted truths that have stood the test of time is absolutely critical if you are to understand, anticipate, and excel in this world.

The following chapters will help you begin building your superstructure, indeed your very own personal Parthenon. As C. S. Lewis suggested, the process will involve a great deal of work, some of which will surprise and certainly challenge you. But as you begin to build with the end in mind, going brick by brick, level by level, you will find yourself (and others) marveling at the results, just as you've marveled at many of the world's best-known superstructures.

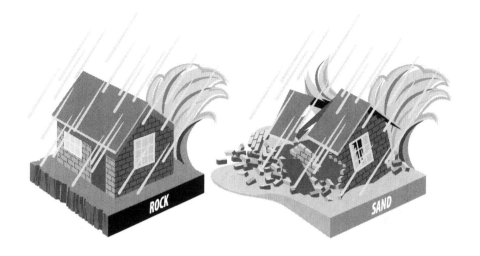

CHAPTER 2

Unifying Principles:
Setting a Solid Foundation

A wise man "built his house upon a rock: And the rain descended, and the floods came, and the winds blew, and beat upon that house; and it fell not: for it was founded upon a rock." A foolish man "built his house upon the sand: And the rain descended, and the floods came, and the winds blew, and beat upon that house; and it fell: And great was the fall of it."

— Adapted from the New Testament, Matthew 7:24-27

During his early years as a business consultant and author, Charles spent considerable time studying Benjamin Franklin's autobiography wherein Franklin describes a carefully devised method for "attaining perfection." Franklin tells of how, at the age of 27, he desired to improve himself and his life by identifying what he considered to be universal principles of truth. The result of his inquiry is what the world now knows as the "Thirteen Virtues of Ben Franklin."

After identifying these principles, Franklin set about on a quest to live all thirteen virtues perfectly before he died. While studying Franklin's life, Charles realized that what Franklin was attempting to do was unify himself with truth by defining those principles he should be valuing most, and then every day for the rest of his life trying to align his performance with these principles.

Drawing from Franklin's lifelong quest, Charles developed an approach for systematically identifying and implementing enduring ideas of truth that he designated as unifying principles. When properly implemented, these unifying principles would provide the foundational power to optimizing productivity in goal planning and in achieving a fulfilled life.

From that moment on, Charles's insight into the power of Unifying Principles served as a functional roadmap throughout his personal and business life. This realization was the beginning of Charles' development of the *Doctrine of Self-Unification*, which will be discussed in greater detail later in chapter 7.

It was during this process of discovery that, on February 3, 1976, Charles was hired as a consultant by a distribution company to work with employees who were not performing as desired by management. And it was his experience with one of these less-than-stellar employees that shaped his entire approach to maximizing personal productivity.

One day the company president called Charles into her office to tell him about an employee she was about to let go due to what she deemed as an unacceptable decline in attitude and productivity over the course of several months. However, she had made the decision to give this employee one final opportunity to change his ways, but only if Charles would consider guiding and helping him one-on-one. Charles accepted her request. The following is Charles's account of what happened over the next weeks and months.

After establishing criteria for success and setting a timetable with the president, I then met with this employee (who I will call Bert) for the first time. It didn't take more than a few seconds to see that Bert clearly did not want to be there. It looked like a hopeless case from the outset. But I sensed a certain fear and vulnerability in Bert which surely stemmed from an acute awareness of his tenuous employment. I remember thinking to myself that this was something I could build on; the fact that he was not so far gone as to still be somewhat in touch with the reality of his situation.

A few minutes into our meeting Bert surprisingly opened up. He freely admitted that his performance had dramatically deteriorated. During this time he had lost faith in his ability to make good decisions, and had squandered the trust of his superiors, along with the confidence of his associates. On top of all of this, he had lost the love and respect of family and friends. These were all compounded by Bert's pride and unwillingness to seek the help he so desperately and obviously needed.

Bert shared how often he would find himself in the wrong place at the wrong time doing the wrong things with the wrong people, but felt powerless to escape the rut and cycle of failure he now found himself in. It was as if he was paralyzed to do anything to help himself.

Bert then expressed how much he loved his children. He had been married and divorced twice, with kids resulting from each marriage; but less than amicable relationships with both ex-wives made it difficult to spend the kind of time with his children that he wanted and they needed. As a result, he felt tremendous guilt and inadequacy as a father.

He went on to describe how out of control he felt, which often resulted in poor judgment and failing to keep commitments. He had become so wrapped up in his personal problems that insubordination to his superiors and indifference to others led often to misjudging their motives and even undermining their efforts.

Filled with such a constant fear of failure and pervasive negativity in his life, Bert was carrying around an enormous amount of self-

loathing, guilt-ridden baggage. It was readily apparent to me that Bert had never given much thought to what he should be valuing most in his life other than his children. He had no direction, no focus, and no purpose—and rarely, if ever, developed or achieved meaningful goals of any kind. He was a "dysfunctional floater" who was completely out of control with the events in his life, resulting in low self-esteem and diminished productivity.

Bert had clearly hit rock bottom, but surprisingly expressed to me a desire to change his life if I felt it wasn't too late. It was then I knew we had a real shot at turning his situation around for the better.

Before ending our first visit, I decided to give Bert an assignment to answer the following question on a sheet of paper:

"What should I be valuing more than anything else in my life?"

He quickly responded with "I love my children more than anything!" I said, "That's a great start." I then handed him a sheet of paper and said, "Write at the top, MY UNIFYING PRINCIPLES, and under this heading write, 'Love my children.'"

I encouraged him to do some soul searching before answering further, then to write his answers on a sheet of paper and bring them to our meeting the following week. I reminded him that the values he would write down should come through self-discovery and not from anyone else, or what he thought others or I would want him to say.

Bert then asked me if there was not some source he could refer to for help in identifying his values and principles. I told him that many people over the course of centuries have drawn on religious and literary works for inspiration and guidance, but I urged him to trust in his own heart and conscience the most when identifying those principles he would use as a guide in future goal planning and living.

Our meeting the following week was a rewarding one to say the least. To my great surprise, Bert had written down nearly two full pages of personal and work-related things he valued most in life. At the top of his list was the love he had for his children. I told him this was a good place to start and to write it down as a principle of action: "Love and care for my children."

We spent the next hour formulating action statements and paragraphs of clarification for each of his values, as well as prioritizing each by order of importance to him. When we were finished, Bert had a well-defined set of unifying principles.

For our next meeting, I assigned Bert to set aside at least fifteen minutes every morning for planning and contemplation on the unifying principles at the very top of his list. During this time he was to visualize bringing his daily performance in line with each principle without exception.

Bert came back the following week so pumped up and beaming with newly found confidence I could hardly believe the transformation. He told me: "Every morning for the past week I have visualized living my most valued principles throughout that day, and I have already seen improvement in the way I think and act about things. Boy, it feels good."

From that day on, Bert took off like an eagle. Over the next several weeks, we would meet periodically, while continuing to develop and monitor progress with the rest of his unifying principles.

Several months after completing my contract with the company, I returned for a follow-up visit. The president said to me: "Charles, I don't know what went on in those sessions, but Bert is doing exceptionally well, so much so that I am going to promote him to a key management position in our company."

A few minutes later I met with Bert. There was no mistaking the confidence, inner peace, and obvious joy that he exuded. After some discussion, he shared with me how in the process of sharing with his second ex-wife the unifying principles he identified, they discovered that they shared many of the same values and were even talking about getting remarried. What a remarkable transformation.

Bert had made the personal discovery that greater fulfillment could be brought about by living in accordance with what he identified as the most important valued priorities in his life. While going through this process, Bert was forced to look at himself through a mirror of reality testing. By identifying what he should value most in life and then aligning his performance with those values, Bert developed a solid foundation for taking greater control of events in his life, with higher self-esteem and increased quality productivity the result. He was in the process of becoming a self-unified person.

Unifying Principles

There are two questions you need to ask yourself when developing your own unifying principles.

1. What do I value most?
2. What should I value most?

In answering the first question, you establish where you are right now in relation to what you believe you value most. The purpose of the second question is to propel you into the realm of Unified Power as you explore what you *should* value most based on truths that have stood the test of time.

Anne Mulcahy, former Chairman and CEO of Xerox once said: "Who you are, and what your values are, what you stand for...they are your anchor, your north star.... You'll find them in your soul."

Everyone has some form of values by which they base their decisions and actions on. Each of our days is filled with multiple mini-decision points that require action based on either a self-directed value system or one that is defined for or imposed on us by others. For many of us, problems arise when we fail to recognize and to systematically define and prioritize our most important values. It all boils down to this simple axiom:

"Control the events in your life, or life will control you."

Throughout history, all the truly great military, political, scientific, academic, and spiritual leaders have possessed a core set of unifying principles that has transformed them from ordinary men and women into peak performers and pillars of strength. By aligning their performance with their core values, they came to personify the very definition of a personal superstructure.

Much in the same way that the Parthenon's upward structure, or entablature, was supported by large pillars that rested on a solid limestone foundation, so your superstructure needs to be built upon a rock-solid foundation of truths that have stood the test of time, truths that remain unchangeable regardless of popular opinion or relativism. These truths, or principles, should shape and guide your every thought, decision, and action on a daily basis.

For most of us, Unifying Principles either come naturally or as a result of upbringing and education. In any case, such principles must be continuously learned and re-learned, applied and re-applied, and perfected over the course of lifetime matriculation. To assist in this process, we will identify in the next chapters those fundamental truths, indeed, the four Unified Power Principles that will function as the cornerstones of your personal , or organizational, superstructure.

CHAPTER 3

Unified Power Principle #1:
Integrity

"I look for three things in hiring people. The first is personal integrity, the second is intelligence, and the third is a high energy level. But, if you don't have the first, the other two will kill you."

— Warren Buffet, CEO, Berkshire Hathaway

A wise religious leader once taught a group of university students the following lesson:

Athens in Greece was once recognized as the great and unique city of the world…. It was not only a seat of government but of learning and commerce, of art and science.

Each young man of Athens, when he reached the age of eighteen, took this oath:

"We will never bring disgrace on this our City by an act of dishonesty or cowardice.

"We will fight for the ideals and sacred things of the City, both alone and with many.

"We will revere and obey the city's laws, and will do our best to incite a like reverence and respect in those above us who are prone to annul them or set them at naught.

"We will strive increasingly to quicken the public sense of civic duty.

"Thus in all these ways we will transmit the City, not lessened, but greater and more beautiful than it was transmitted to us." (Adapted from the Ephebic Oath, cf. Phillip Harding, ed. and *trans.,* Translated Documents of Greece and Rome 2: From the End of the Peloponnesian War to the Battle of Ipsus *[Cambridge: Cambridge University Press, 1985], pp. 122-35 [109A].)*

That solemn commitment and its subsequent expression in the lives of Athenian young men helped transform Athens into "the cultural capital of the world." Indeed, the very superstructure of Athens at that time was built upon the principle of integrity, which we define as:

Dealing honestly and fairly with oneself and others in an unbroken state of moral uprightness.

One of the most important aspects of integrity within a superstructure is its ability to secure trust. "Trust is having total confidence in the integrity, ability, and good character of another." (*Webster's Dictionary.*)

Early in his career, Greg participated in a mandatory "Mission, Vision, Values" meeting. His company had invested a considerable amount of money and time in preparation for this one-day event. The objectives were simple: to create a new culture and establish core values. An off-site location was secured and employees from across the country were flown in. The company spared no expense or effort.

The meeting started off with canned presentations by the CEO and senior management read from Teleprompters. Carefully orchestrated multi-media presentations coupled with individual and group exercises filled the rest of the day.

During one of the exercises, large 4' x 4' white canvas boards were distributed to tables where six to eight employees were seated. Each table was given the assignment to describe what they felt about a value that was assigned to them. Some of the words included *fun, creative, hard work,* and *best.* One team was assigned the word *integrity.*

Each team was then given twenty minutes to complete the assignment. When the time was up, a spokesperson from each team was asked to explain their findings to the entire group in the form of words or drawings on their canvas board. One by one each team presented its masterpiece until finally it was Team Integrity's turn. Its team members were silent. Their canvas was blank. They were unable to come up with a single way to write, draw, or explain the assigned concept. It was an awkward moment for the team, as well as for many in the room, especially the executives who were so determined to establish "core values."

In the weeks that followed, each of the large canvas motifs was displayed on the walls throughout the corporate offices. It didn't take long before everyone noticed the stark white emptiness of the "integrity" canvas.

Whether by accident or design, this particular canvas was placed on a wall right between the offices of the CEO and a senior vice-president. The significance of this juxtaposition was not lost on many in the company, especially those in middle management.

Part of the problem why this core values exercise failed to achieve buy-in was that prior to this meeting, confidence in senior management's ability to make the right decisions and do the right thing was already waning. For years the upper echelon would announce a major organizational initiative, put up clever banners and posters, and launch company-wide objectives, only to act the complete opposite in how they treated employees, suppliers, and customers. Not surprisingly, at the time of this retreat the company was dealing with very low employee morale and was struggling financially.

For the next few months following the Mission, Vision, Values meeting, many employees took a wait-and-see attitude. Almost everyone in the company wanted to see the called-for values succeed, but there was still great skepticism and distrust. Unfortunately, it wasn't long before many of the promises made at the meeting were forgotten, the values-based initiatives were abandoned, and executives were back to their "normal" way of doing business. This resulted in the company's culture, morale, and financial wellbeing dropping to even lower levels than before the meeting. Within six months, the morale of the company was in utter shambles and the company was on the brink of bankruptcy.

Integrity begins and ends with trust earned not by promises but by action. In any relationship, professional or personal, when integrity is lost, so too is trust. And when there is no trust, no amount of hyperbole or feigned benevolence will ever be able to restore belief and confidence.

In the 1990s James Patterson and Peter Kim set out to take the moral pulse of the United States. Using state-of-the-art research techniques, they conducted the largest survey of private morals ever undertaken to unearth and quantify the personal ethics, values, and beliefs of the time.

This comprehensive survey disclosed that the number-one cause for decline in society was a general lack of ethics, among other things. Sadly, little has changed in the years since, and we see today the effects of a lack of integrity playing out every day in institutions and interpersonal relationships. Countless examples come to mind as we write, but were we to list them, they would be completely outdated and replaced by a new batch of even greater violations and scoundrels before this book goes to press.

It seems that every time an individual or an institution makes headlines for what is invariably a lapse of integrity, there is an endless stream of commentary on our need to mend our ways, which inevitably has little effect. In an effort to put into practice the principle of integrity, let's examine six essential characteristics that are present in an individual possessing impeccable integrity.

1. A person of integrity keeps all commitments.

As a young boy Charles worked in his father's grocery store where he learned many valuable lessons from his father. One of the most important was to never make a commitment to anyone unless you are sure you can keep it.

Charles remembers his father saying, "Son, a man is no better than his word. Your word is your bond. Be a man of integrity. Never at any time allow an exception to occur on any commitment you make to people you associate with."

Abraham Lincoln once borrowed a book with a promise to return it in the same condition. A rain shower destroyed the book before he could return it. For the next few months Lincoln, then only about fourteen years old, hired himself out doing odd jobs and hard labor until he had enough money to replace the damaged book with a new one.

A person of impeccable integrity keeps all commitments in order to build unwavering trust with others. If you promise to be somewhere at 9 A.M., then be there five minutes early. If you quote a price and promise a level of service, then honor that price and over-deliver on the service.

By being consistent in keeping *all* commitments, even seemingly small and insignificant ones, you will build greater confidence in your own abilities that will be rewarded by the trust others will place in you.

2. A person of integrity never exaggerates the truth.

What is it that makes the truth so elusive? Think of how many relationship problems, financial hardships, and feelings of general discontentment could be avoided if only the truth, and nothing but the truth, were extolled openly and candidly.

A young woman who had worked for a few years in Silicon Valley found it necessary to relocate her family to the Midwest. Lacking confidence in her credentials and breadth of experience, which most would have viewed as quite limited, she embellished her resume by taking credit for contributions with which she had been only minimally involved.

In a matter of time, she was able to land a job managing a small but talented group of seasoned software engineers. However, after just a few short months it became apparent to her superiors and subordinates that she was in over her head trying to oversee an operation she actually knew little about. After some additional investigation by her boss, it was readily apparent that her resume had been padded with misrepresentations, half-truths, and a few fabrications. Somewhat surprisingly, the young woman was demoted rather than fired. But during her time with this company, she never fully recovered from her lapse in judgment and lack of integrity.

It can be tempting to embellish or fudge the truth to win the praise of others, get off the hook, or pad your numbers; but such behavior does not secure trust in yourself or others, and will always catch up to you sooner or later in one way or another.

3. A person of integrity is free of any form of deception.

"Lincoln could not rest for an instant under the consciousness that he had, even unwittingly, defrauded anybody." (*Abe Lincoln's Stories and Speeches*, J.B. McClure, 1894, p. 27.)

An advertising executive for a mid-sized magazine publisher found himself in an awkward position one day when he went to pick up a check from one of his accounts; for some strange reason the check had been made out to him rather than to his company. He had felt underappreciated and underpaid at work, and adding to this were the increasing demands of a growing family. Although he had always felt he was a man of integrity, he soon found himself at his bank, depositing the check in his account. He convinced himself this act of embezzlement was justified, and when questions arose at work about where the payment was, he simply said the advertiser was running late.

This cycle repeated itself for several months, until his supervisor began insisting that the advertiser bring its account current before it ran any more ads. Before long, the deception was uncovered, the man lost his job, criminal charges were filed, and his wife divorced him. Although he had been able to deceive himself and others for a time, he learned the hard way that truth invariably surfaces, often to the extreme discomfort of those who have tried to suppress it.

Integrity is free from the so-called realities of perception and deception. It ignores blurred lines, bleeding boundaries, and shades of gray. It does not rely on the magician's slight of hand or the smooth-talker's craft of words. It wears no mask and hides behind no curtain, but stands boldly and confidently without makeup or mask before any crowd in all circumstances.

4. A person of integrity does not lie, steal, or cheat.

At the end of a self-unification training session in Washington D.C., the chief financial officer of a company came up to Charles with a question. He said:

> I have been in this position with my company for two years. A few days ago the CEO called me into his office to discuss the financial status of the company. He showed me how certain numbers could be adjusted in a way that no one else in the company would know except the two of us. He also explained how this would be a benefit to the company. I asked for some time to study the numbers and think it over. The next day I told him I had serious reservations concerning his proposal. Then he insisted that I work this through with him. I asked for more time but he has given me an ultimatum. I have to give him an answer tomorrow. I have a high paying job. He has offered to increase my stock options. I have a family to feed. What is your counsel, Charles?

Charles responded by saying, "When you wrote your unifying principles today, were any of them related to integrity?" "Yes," the CFO said. "I put down: Be honest in all my doings."

"Then you know what you have to do," replied Charles. "Pack up your bags and get out! You're better off being out of a job than ending up in prison." The CFO gave a sigh of relief and said, "I know this is the action I have to take. I just needed a nudge in the right direction."

Shakespeare wrote, "This above all: to thy own self be true, and it must follow, as the night the day, Thou cans't not then be false to any man." (Hamlet.)

5. A person of integrity forgives others when offended and, when possible, strives with compassion to help strengthen the offender's integrity.

One of the most deleterious behaviors in achieving quality productivity and living a balanced life is the inability to forgive when offended.

One who harbors a petty or serious grievance, takes personal offense, blames others for how he or she feels, tries to enforce unenforceable rules, and makes false judgments with unbridled pride is not dealing honestly with self and others. This person is living an incongruous life that is grounded within a *broken* state of moral uprightness.

The ideal response, which is not always easy to do, is to forgive the offense spontaneously at the moment it happens. There is unifying power in forgiving when done the right way. As an example, Charles shares the following:

One of the most valuable lessons I learned from my father was not only to forgive when wronged by someone, but to strive to help strengthen the wrong doer's integrity.

Late one night our telephone rang. It was the police. The officer said to my father, "Milo, a thief is breaking into your grocery store through the back entrance. I am ready to apprehend him." As dad was beginning to pull on his trousers, he said, "Officer, let me take care of this. I will be there shortly. Watch him till I get there, then quietly slip away." Although concerned for my father's safety, the officer nevertheless complied.

When my dad pulled up to the back of the store, he saw the door open. Now out of his car, he came face to face with the thief who was carrying an armful of groceries to his old clunker.

Recognizing the man, Dad called out, "Ed, why are you doing this?" Embarrassed and with a bowed head, Ed answered, "My family is hungry, and I have no money to buy food for them."

My father said, "Here, let me help you." They put the stolen groceries in the car. Then my father said, "Now, let's go get some more. You have a large family."

Once the car was filled with food, my father said, "Ed, I think it's time you and I have a talk. It's wrong to steal anything from anybody, even when in desperate need. It can get you and your family in a lot of trouble. The next time you are in need, come to me. I will do what I can to help you."

A predictable characteristic found in a person of impeccable integrity is that this person forgives at the spur-of-the moment when offended and, when possible and appropriate, strives with compassion to strengthen the offender's integrity. This is what happened that late evening outside Charles's father's grocery store.

6. A person of integrity is in close touch with reality.

Most people are prone to think more of themselves or their accomplishments than they have any right to. Someone once said: "Funny how a man generally can do more than he thinks he can, and almost always does less than he thinks he does."

But, as demonstrated earlier, rationalization can easily remove you from reality when you seek to justify inappropriate behaviors or sub-par performance. When you climb down from your lofty pedestal and look into your own Don Quixote mirror—and see *you* for who you really are—it can be both sobering and frightening.

The paradox of mankind is that truth is the only principle that can truly set us free, but it is that very truth that we so often try to avoid, abdicate, or abuse. What should come easily and naturally to each of us can become perverted and confusing unless constant vigilance and concerted effort are exercised.

Integrity is the consistent practice of dealing honestly and fairly with oneself and others in an unbroken state of moral uprightness. A person of integrity keeps all commitments, never exaggerates the truth; is free from any form of deception; does not lie, steal, or cheat; forgives others when offended (and when possible responds with compassion to help strengthen the offender's integrity); and is in close touch with reality.

Such a person is predictable in securing the prized reward of trust in self and others.

There are countless good, honest, ethical individuals in the world who, not unlike the youth of Athens, are fully committed to living lives of integrity. Then there are those who, much like some of Greg's associates, seem to draw a blank when faced with circumstances that require them to do what is right. An old Christian hymn admonishes us to "Choose the right when the choice is placed before you." For some, doing so is instinctive—they would never think to do otherwise. For others, the instinct is to follow the path of expediency or least resistance. Both history and each day's news makes clear which is the right path to follow, without deviation and what the consequences are for those who do not.

The Unified Power Principle of Integrity means being honest and truthful in every motive, word, and action. It is the first cornerstone of your enduring superstructure that will stand the test of time.

Unified Power Steps

1. For twenty-four hours, test your integrity by being completely honest in everything you say, paying close attention to white lies, fuzzy characterizations, or overstated performance. Keep up a running log, and at the end of the twenty-four hours, review where you failed and succeeded in your "honest" communications.

2. For one week (Monday–Sunday), keep 100 percent of all your commitments to family, friends, associates, and customers. Be on time to every meeting and for dinner. Follow through on every personal promise or deadline. Do not allow an exception to occur as if your life depended on it. Keep track of your performance and use your failures and successes to make improvements and build confidence.

3. Identify one person whom you consider to have impeccable integrity, and list at least five characteristics of that person. Evaluate your own performance to see how it stacks up against this person. Commit to make any necessary changes for which you see a need.

CHAPTER 4

Unified Power Principle #2:
Faith

"Where there is no faith in the future, there is no power in the present."

— *David MacLennan*

Imagine a world where you lacked any certainty about the future. At the most basic level, you would go to bed unsure of whether the sun would rise tomorrow. You would go on a trip wondering if your spouse and children would be there to greet you when you returned. You would go to work not knowing if you'd get your next paycheck. Such scenarios may seem rather far-fetched to most of us, but they point to how much we each rely on faith—in ourselves, in others, in predictabilities that give meaning to all that we do day-to-day. Sometimes, the word *faith* is viewed largely in religious terms; but, in its broader sense, **faith is the assurance that anticipated events will occur and that desired results can be achieved.**

If we pause for a moment and think about the role faith plays in our lives, most of us would be surprised at its often overlooked role. Faith's power to motivate us to do everything from getting out of bed in the morning to putting effort into our various responsibilities—and everything in between—is ever-present.

Without faith, anticipated events and desired results are little more than vague notions of what you hope to achieve. With faith, these vague notions are transformed into **goals** — events you seek to achieve and feel empowered to accomplish. Whether we are conscious of its power or not, it is only by and through faith that any task or goal, large or small, can be accomplished.

Let's say that you have been assigned to serve as leader of a team composed of nine other members. Your assignment is to determine why sales of a critical product have dropped 16 percent in the past six weeks, and to then develop and present a strategic plan on how you will convert that loss into a 30 percent gain within six months.

Without faith in yourself, your colleagues, and your company, this assignment would seem hopeless and unattainable. But if you look for evidences of faith based on your experience and past performance, you likely will see that this result can be achieved. You will believe, even know, that you and your team can develop and implement the necessary changes to bring about this goal by the project's deadline.

You will recognize that your team members are diversified in skill and experience. This will give you confidence in each person's ability to contribute with competency and professionalism. Such trust and belief in yourself and in others secures the assurance of a desired result and is an example of faith in action.

Each of us should often be in the process of contemplating our past, present, and future. We learn and grow in the here and now by drawing on knowledge from the past, while attempting to anticipate and control events in the future. It is through systematic, anticipatory thought and planning of unknowns that we begin to become masters, not servants, of our present and future. This is done by and through the Unified Power Principle of Faith.

There are three basic levels of faith, with the first level functioning as a vital, preliminary step to the other two. These levels are **Belief, Faith,** and **Super Faith.**

Belief

Belief, at its most basic level, involves a measure of trust in a person, thing, or anticipated event. It is a hopeful agreement of acceptance that helps secure confidence in something or someone.

For example, if you are supervising a brand new employee, you are likely operating from a passive belief that he or she can be depended on and will be able to perform the tasks they've been assigned. But if you are teaming up with a seasoned professional with whom you've achieved major objectives over the years, you will have a much more active sense of belief in what the two of you can accomplish.

Belief always comes before a person can begin to exercise any type of active faith. It is the flame that ignites the fuse of faith.

Building on trust, belief is an essential catalyst that lifts you up from mere desire or hope toward the realm of faith and action. Remember, one of the greatest teachers of all taught, "If thou canst believe, all things are possible to him that believeth" (New Testament, Mark 9:23).

Faith

A person cannot possess faith without first having belief; however, a person can believe and still lack the faith necessary to produce desired results. Unlike belief, faith is active, not passive. It converts belief into real, actionable power. It is the moving cause and driving force for action in humankind.

All the believing, intention, and planning, in your life would be useless without the sufficient faith to transform these into action. Without the driving force of faith, your mind and body would be in a stalemate.

Super Faith

If belief is the flame that lights the fuse of faith, then faith is the fuse that launches the rocket of super faith into the realm of all possibility. Super faith is more than just anticipating events and taking action; it is about bringing these anticipated events into your immediate and direct control. When exercised correctly, super faith activates a level of trust, confidence and anticipatory planning that brings future events and desired outcomes into the present so they can be acted upon now.

Let's reexamine the three conditions for controlling events presented in the Introduction of this book as they relate to these three levels of faith.

1. There are events you should control, but you don't.

For many reasons, including fear, doubt, laziness, or procrastination, there are many important events that just do not materialize in your life. However, most of these failures can be overcome by applying the principles of faith and effective planning.

Planning is bringing events into the present so something can be done about them now. In chapters that follow, we will not only give you the tools for effective planning but will share with you a method of prioritizing anticipated events to be brought under control that will give you the highest payoff at work and in your personal life.

2. There are events you think you can control, but you can't.

When a person is out of touch with reality or the hard facts, there can be no true faith. Remember, faith is the assurance that anticipated events will occur and that desired results can be achieved. In short, faith is the assurance that a worthy goal can be accomplished.

When was the last time you committed to an unreasonable goal, only to discover it could not be achieved, no matter how hard you tried? Did you feel disappointment, frustration, a loss of confidence or self-esteem, maybe even anger?

Imagine yourself trying to reach a long distance destination late at night, utterly exhausted after driving all day. Most of us have been down that sleepy road before. Before you left on your journey, you committed yourself to a goal or outcome you thought you could effectively control but could not.

Your brain and your body begin to demand rest. To continue further presents a real danger to yourself and others. In this scenario, you have tried to enforce an unenforceable rule on yourself for an event you ultimately cannot control. You started with a false assurance of faith that your goal could be achieved, but the reality is that the laws of nature will not allow it.

As you think through and develop your goals during the process of anticipatory planning, it is important to be realistic about what you can control—and therefore achieve. In other words, "Keep it real!"

3. There are events you think you cannot control, but you can.

Shakespeare said it best: "Our doubts are traitors and oft times make us lose the good we might win by fearing to attempt." Doubt and fear are the antithesis of faith and are paralyzing agents.

When President John F. Kennedy boldly stated, "We will put a man on the moon before the end of the decade," people wondered how such an incredible feat in such a short period of time could be achieved. Yet NASA went to work with unparalleled faith, both in Kennedy's vision and in its ability to perform a manned lunar landing and, more important, a safe return to earth. There was no room for doubt or fear.

On July 20, 1969, eight short years after President Kennedy set forth that very ambitious goal, Neil Armstrong and Buzz Aldrin landed on the moon, proving that what was once thought impossible and improbable was in fact a reality.

William James, who contributed significantly to modern psychology, wrote that what most people achieve out of their potential could be placed on the tip of their little finger.

It is in overcoming this third condition of controlling events that is found the culmination of belief and faith as demonstrated in the true genius and power of super faith.

Dorothea Brande offered this wise counsel:

All that is necessary to break the spell of inertia and frustration is this: act as if it were impossible to fail. That is the talisman, the formula, the command of right-about-face that turns us from failure toward success.

At first glance, it might seem that trying to control events one cannot control is at odds with reality. For those who possess mere belief or simple faith, attempting to control such events would probably put them out of touch with reality. But all great progress, invention, creation, and innovation grow out of an unyielding and undaunted defiance of what the vast majority view as uncontrollable.

Many people thought Columbus, Edison, and the Wright Brothers were crazy for believing they could control events that were uncontrollable. Those who doubted were proven wrong.

In the face of the crowd the undaunted few never say never until their desired outcome is achieved. These are the people who do not listen to the skeptics who say, "It can't be done."

Edwin Chapin stated, "Skepticism has not founded empires, established principles, or changed the world's heart. The great doers of history have always been men of faith." They are people like Florence Nightingale, Nicola Tessla, and Ghandi, people who believed they could change the world. In our own time, we have witnessed such an example we may now take for granted in Bill Gates, who believed that a personal computer in every office and home would one day be a reality at a time when such an ambitious vision was beyond the realm of imagination and possibility.

These people, and others like them, are the individual superstructures that have helped change the course of events in our world through their super faith. They possessed the ability to focus on and accomplish their most vital priorities in producing optimal results that the rest of the world believed could not be accomplished.

Early in their lives, each of these visionaries may have appeared to be ordinary people like you and me—with one noticeable difference. They each had a vision of what they knew they could accomplish—and they never let go and never gave up, often against all odds, until their lofty goals were accomplished.

The eleven CEOs chronicled in the book *Good to Great* lifted their companies with "unwavering faith that they would prevail, regardless of difficulties that often stood in their way." (Jim Collins, *Good to Great* [New York: HarperCollins, 2001], p. 13) Whether they knew it or not (and a good guess would be that they did) these CEOs realized the key to success was in controlling anticipated events others thought could not be controlled. With their vision, mission, and values clearly defined, these leaders generated positive fields of energy yielding incredible results by harnessing the power of super faith.

Let's now bring the principle of faith into the world of everyday life.

Evidences That Empower Faith

There are four steps in the development of faith, indeed super faith, that will help empower you to achieve your intended results through the control of events and circumstances.

1. Think of past achievements that relate to your goal.

A key element in developing the assurance of faith is evidence. If you can build enough evidence within yourself that you can achieve a worthy goal, then it will be realized. The noted psychiatrist Ari Kiev said, "The successful life is a succession of successful days."

As a young boy growing up in a small community, Rene watched the local high school band perform in a holiday parade. He became enamored with the row of trumpet players blasting out the tunes. For four years he begged his parents, unsuccessfully, for a trumpet. Finally, in the ninth grade his dream was realized. He took trumpet lessons and practiced faithfully. He tried out for first chair in the junior high band and got it. Later on in high school he tried out for first chair in the band, and held that position for all four years.

Upon graduating from high school Rene was admitted to a noted university that was acclaimed as having the finest marching band west of the Mississippi.

Rene soon found himself trying out for first chair along with 28 other trumpet players, most of whom had been first chair in their high school bands. Building on his earlier success and the evidence that he could achieve his desired goals, coupled with a lot of determination, practice, and faith, Rene took first chair.

From that time forward Rene earned first chair in all other bands and orchestras he tried out for. In early adulthood Rene had the distinct privilege of studying at The Hague conservatory of music in Holland under Theo Lanen, the acclaimed principal trumpet player of the Philharmonic Symphony of The Hague.

Rene found that one success in an endeavor could be layered upon a previous success on which still other successes could be layered.

Although Rene eventually pursued a profession unrelated to music and the trumpet, he had become empowered by past evidences of faith that worthy future goals could be achieved. And they were. He enjoyed a highly successful career as an educator and businessman throughout the decades that followed. "The successful life is a succession of successful days as we build upon our past achievements."

A useful way to ensure future success is to write down a "Victory List" of every achievement, great or small, that you have already achieved. No matter the project or the goal, this simple writing activity can dramatically increase your confidence to achieve by providing you with added assurances of faith, based on evidence of successful past performance, which are predictors of desired results in the future.

2. Visualize performing the necessary steps to achieve your goal.

In order to activate your faith as a principle of power, you must focus on the idea that "thought generates action." This particularly applies when committing to an anticipated event or outcome you hope to bring in control.

At a lunch break during a training session in Chicago, Charles asked several participants at one of the tables to comment on an important goal they were in the process of achieving. The last person to speak was an astute 24-year-old woman. She said: "I want to tell you about a high-priority personal goal that is my passion. I am a professional archer. In national competition I recently shot a score of 297 out of a possible 300 using 60 arrows." That meant she had hit a near-perfect bull's-eye with almost every arrow.

Charles then asked her, "How did you accomplish such an incredible feat?" She replied, "I have one of the greatest archery instructors in the nation. As you would put it, Charles, I have been standing on the shoulders of a giant." Then she added, "And I practice three hours a day."

Curious, Charles questioned her on how she found the time in her busy work and personal life to dedicate three hours at the range, to which she responded:

"Oh no! A good deal of that time I am going through a process called visualization. On the range my instructor guides me with clarity on specific movements, actions, and attitudes required to land a perfect bull's-eye. But much of my success can be attributed to when I'm away from the range, where I spend a lot of time visualizing every movement and every action."

Maxwell Maltz, in his book *Psycho-Cybernetics*, stated, "The moment you experience an event vividly in your imagination it is recorded as experience."

The process of visualization, when done correctly and consistently, is an evidence of faith helping to secure assurance that a desired result can be achieved. Whatever the result, if you can properly imagine yourself performing the necessary steps to achieving it through positive and concentrated thought, you can transform almost any worthy goal into a desired outcome.

3. Selectively identify with and learn from worthy models that have achieved.

Years ago Bandura and Dollard introduced the principle of "imitation psychology," meaning "we learn by imitating the behaviors and attitudes of what we see in other people."

A little girl will watch how her mother cares for a baby sister, and then try to feed, change the diaper, and dress her dolly in like manner. A young boy will imitate his father driving the family car with his toy cars.

People of all ages continue to learn by imitating what they see selected models do. As a child matures into adulthood, his or her stable of options to imitate increases. Unfortunately, many people follow one of two roads of imitation. Some huddle together like sheep as they mindlessly follow the flock, lacking any independent thought or action. As a result, they become carbon copies of their environment, which leads to unrealized potential and a life lacking in significant achievement. Others pattern their lives after models that often turn out to be unethical or immoral business leaders, politicians, sports heros, rock stars or celebrities.

Gratefully, there are still many people across all walks of life who are pillars of success and who have achieved what they have by following principles of integrity and faith. One such a person is Dr. Allen E. Bergin, a world-renowned clinical psychologist.

As a young man Allen set his moral compass toward becoming a devout Christian. He spent his entire life developing and living with impeccable integrity, embracing humility, showing forth love, and maintaining faith in himself and God.

Throughout his life Dr. Bergin selectively identified with and learned all he could from professional and religious models who had excelled both personally and professionally. Early on he sought for and emulated the examples of giants in his field of study to help achieve his long-range goal of becoming one of the leading research clinical psychologists in his field.

He received his doctorate under the tutelage of Albert Bandura, who to this day is the most read research clinical psychologist in the world. Every year for decades after completing his education, Dr. Bergin met with his mentor to exchange and validate ideas.

After receiving his Ph.D. at Stanford University, Dr. Bergin did post-graduate studies for one year with the noted psychologist Carl Rogers, who was one of the first to introduce religious values into the field of psychology.

Dr. Bergin would later become a distinguished professor at Columbia University for nearly ten years, and for more than three decades played a key leadership role in the Department of Psychology at Brigham Young University.

Among his noteworthy contributions has been advancing the integration of religious values into the field of psychology. He has published ten books and over a hundred professional articles, and has been honored nationally and internationally with the most distinguished awards in his profession. Dr. Bergin not only selectively identified with models to achieve his worthy goals, but also became a model himself to countless students.

But you say, "I have no models or mentors that are accessible to me." Granted, such noble and successful men and women like Dr. Bergin are not your run-of-the-mill people. They are often not accessible to rub shoulders with, let alone be tutored under.

However, no matter who you are, where you are, or what your status is in life, there are people not far from your reach who have achieved and are achieving great things. They may not be a noted figure of the day, but if you look close enough they are all around you. They can be your boss, an associate, a neighbor, a friend of a friend, or even a family member. Reach out to them. You might be surprised just how accessible and willing they are to share their experience and wisdom with you.

If for any reason you can't readily identify with or gain access to a selected model, then look for other examples on the Internet or in the many written biographies that are available. By reading and studying the lives of people who have already achieved, you can learn what it took for them to accomplish what they did.

Once you have carefully selected your model (past or present), gather all the biographical data you can find on this person. Try to enter their inner world and seek to understand the "how" and the "why" of their failures and successes. Study this person's life with the goal of becoming so intimately acquainted with them that you begin to understand their thought processes, and why and how they did what they did. When finished choose another model and repeat the process.

What does all this have to do with developing super faith? By speaking with or studying the lives of those who have already excelled, there are at least two evidences of faith that offer useful direction:

1. The qualities and attributes of the model you are trying to emulate will be passed on to you directly, or indirectly, through the knowledge, skills, and wisdom this person demonstrated. The fact that they achieved what they did, in many cases in the face of insurmountable obstacles, will greatly strengthen your resolve, confidence, and trust that you can achieve your own desired results.

2. Based on your model's achievements, you will begin to believe and experience a flow of energy and inspiration that will help you produce outcomes beyond your wildest imagination.

   Say to yourself, "If this person was able to excel in making a worthy contribution, so can I."

A word of caution: Always take great care in the person you select to be your mentor or model.

The ancient Greek philosopher Socrates one day entered into a dialogue with Hippocrates, who announced that he planned to become a student of Protagoras. Knowing that Protagoras was a Sophist who engaged in misleading arguments and deception, Socrates began to question: "What will Protagoras make of you?"

With a blush, Hippocrates answered, "I suppose he will make a Sophist of me."

"Are you not ashamed at having to appear in the character of the Sophists?"

"Indeed, Socrates, to confess the truth, I am."

"I wonder whether you know what you are doing?"

"What am I doing?"

"You are going to commit your soul to the care of a man whom you call a Sophist. And yet I hardly think that you know what a Sophist is . . . whether the thing to which you commit yourself be good or evil." (*Great Books of the Western World: The Dialogues of Plato*, vol. 7, pp, 39-40.)

No mentor or model you select will ever be perfectly self-unified without flaw or blemish, but there are clearly those who are more worthy and deserving of your admiration and emulation than others. Even so, it stands to reason that you will need to selectively internalize, adapt, and apply only that knowledge and those skills and attributes displayed by your model that conform to truths that have stood the test of time.

4. Place trust in a power higher than yourself.

It is undeniable that there are forces and influences at work in the universe much greater than can be seen by the naked eye. These forces can either work for you or against you, depending on the level and degree of your faith. If approached and understood correctly, such forces can prove the greatest power and moving cause for action in your life.

Most great leaders achieve by understanding that belief in their own abilities is underscored by a faith and power beyond themselves. One of the main differences between all great achievers and most average people is that achievers know how to tap into this power and convert it into actionable results.

Faith, when based in an entity or purpose greater than self, is the strongest and purest form of affirmation, inspiration, and motivation any human can experience. It does not feel fear, only hope. It does not know doubt, only possibility. Whether this force is spiritual, metaphysical, transcendental, supernatural, real, or perceived, it is the power that stirs imagination, generates creativity and motivates to action.

And it will be a key cornerstone in your personal superstructure.

Unified Power Steps

1. Create a "Victory List" of your past and recent achievements that relate to a current goal. Write down key steps/processes you undertook that could be used to achieve your current (and future) goals.

2. Take time every day (in the shower, on the way to work, in bed before you go to sleep) to visualize yourself performing the steps to achieve your goals. (In Chapter 11 you will receive more specific guidelines on how to use the power of visualization in achieving your goals.)

3. Selectively identify with a successful role model who has achieved. Contact this person and arrange for a conversation in person or over the phone. If the person you select is not available, read their biography, study how they achieved, and then apply those same principles to your goals.

4. Place trust in a power higher than yourself on a daily basis. Draw upon this higher power through daily meditation, reflection, or prayer to give you guidance and inspiration in how to accomplish your valued goals. And remember the old saying, still holds true, "Pray as if everything depends on God and work as if everything depends on you".

CHAPTER 5

Unified Power Principle #3:
Love

"Love is the magic that transforms all things into power and beauty. It brings plenty out of poverty, power out of weakness, loveliness out of deformity, sweetness out of bitterness, light out of darkness, and produces all blissful conditions out of its own substantial but indefinable essence."

— *James Allen*

Through decades of teaching unifying principles all over the world, the principle of love has appeared most often as people's highest of all unifying principles. In fact, many specifically designate the love of God as their number-one unifying principle, followed closely by love of family.

Throughout history love has been responsible for the highest of achievements and joys, and the deepest of disappointments and sorrows. It is a powerful force that has inspired the best and worst of human behavior throughout history.

As we begin exploring the role of love in our personal superstructure, it is important to give serious consideration to the word that has inspired more songs, poems, letters, and books than perhaps any other word. **Love is a heart-felt regard or devotion toward another person, oneself, or any other material or immaterial aspect of life.** Love tends to find its greatest fulfillment in our bonding with those to whom we are most meaningfully connected, such as parents, spouses, children, and friends. For many, the all-encompassing love of God is the most meaningful and motivating form of devotion we experience.

The highest expressions of love, like super faith, tap into supernal and supernatural forces. From love stems the passion, devotion, and aspiration from which all meaningful achievement springs. In its purest and simplest form, love embodies and engenders interest, respect, and genuine concern for our self, for others, and for the divine. For love to have its desired effect as a Unified Power Principle, it must encompass all three of these forms.

Love of Self

Malcomb Forbes once said: "Too many people overvalue what they are not and undervalue what they are." Conversely, a moralist stated: "I would tell you to love your neighbor as yourself, but I don't think anybody could stand that much natural affection." For some, loving themselves comes easily and naturally. For others, finding that love for self is almost impossible. And for most of us in the middle, finding the balance between these two views is a lifelong challenge.

Love of self is not about being narcissistic or egocentric but about having self-respect, a sense of worth, and personal integrity. Loving yourself involves understanding who you are and who you are not. It's about recognizing your unique contribution and achieving your full potential by valuing your talents and abilities in terms of what you have to offer those around you and the world as a whole.

Love of self is more about attitude than platitude. It has nothing to do with what is fair or right. Life is what you take from it and make of it. If you are in an unhappy relationship or a dead-end job, whose fault is that? You may not have control over others or your job, but there is one thing you do have complete control over and that is your attitude.

If you don't love the person you've become, then start becoming the person you want to be. If you hate your job, then try changing your attitude and taking steps to improve your work environment. If that doesn't work, change your job. Love yourself enough to take control of events in your life, whether they are unacceptable conditions or desired future outcomes, and begin to experience greater fulfillment and joy from your life, relationships, and career.

Let's reflect for a minute on the story of Bert in chapter 2. Here was a man who was about as miserable and low as one can get. In fact, he was to the point of self-loathing, knowing the kind of man, father, and employee he had become. He had no direction or focus, and he saw no way out of his predicament. He was so unfulfilled in his personal and professional life that he was near the point of self-destructing in both.

In Bert's case, his belief in God and the love he had for his children were not enough to lift him out of his spiral of despair. It was only when Bert started to believe in *himself* and realize his self-worth by identifying what he valued most in life that he began to see value and purpose in his existence. Only when he began to love himself enough to make a change was he able to develop higher self-esteem and begin to contribute at a higher level.

Charles Lochner wrote:

I may be able to speak with great wisdom and understanding but if I do not love myself, then I understand nothing.

I may talk a good game. I might know a lot about life but if I do not know that I am loved — then I know nothing.

I may be a person of strong faith. Be able to believe with certainty, but if I do not believe in myself — then I believe in nothing.

I may be a person who is always giving, always caring about others' needs — but if I do this, because I can't allow myself to need — then my caring is crippled — it does me no good.

I love myself when I am patient, when I can be quiet with waiting; not rushing my joy nor denying my pain.

I am my own friend — with kindness for free — I own what I am; my anger and hurt; my laughter and love they never own me.

Although my life may be fragile with failure — I am not afraid. I do not hold on to what has gone wrong — for me living is now and love is today.

Love for ourselves is made up of the following forms of love:

Physical Love involves always respecting and valuing who you are by taking pride in your heritage or ethnicity and sharing it with others. It means treating your body with respect and not damaging it with harmful substances, caring for it through proper exercise and nutrition, and taking a measure of pride in how you look. How you present yourself to others is an outward expression of an inner beauty and conviction of self-love.

Mental Love involves filling your mind with creative ideas, visualizing success, learning out of the best books, maintaining a positive mental attitude, keeping your mind free of unnecessary clutter, having clean thoughts and omitting bad ones, and not allowing negativity, self-loathing, or fear to handicap your disposition or actions.

Emotional Love involves being honest with yourself, controlling your fears and insecurities, accepting vulnerability, allowing yourself to love and be loved, being open to and accepting of constructive criticism, exploring worthy desires, living with optimism, smiling, and looking for the good in all things and people (including yourself!).

Spiritual Love involves seeking and acknowledging a higher purpose in life, yielding to the greater good, letting your inner light shine, believing in your divine nature, controlling selfish aspirations, listening to that inner voice inside that whispers truth, seeking inner peace and power, sharing talents, and giving more than receiving.

Ultimately, spiritual love involves kindling a light within and then transmitting that light into the lives of others.

It is impossible to experience the full measure of love in all its forms without first loving yourself. No one will ever enjoy high self-esteem and quality productivity while pretending to be somebody they are not or doing something they do not truly enjoy. By taking a greater interest in who you are and what you want and then aligning your performance with what you value most, you will set yourself on a course of greater love in all aspects of your life.

Love of Others

An old Jewish folktale demonstrates the love we should have toward others.

There were once two brothers who farmed together. They shared equally in all of the work and split the harvest evenly. Each had his own storehouse. One of the brothers was married and had a large family. The other brother was single.

One day the single brother thought to himself: "It is not fair that we divide the grain so evenly. My brother has many mouths to feed, while I have but one. I know what I will do! I will take a sack of grain from my storehouse each evening and put it in my brother's storehouse." So each night when it was dark, he carefully carried a sack of grain and put it in his brother's storehouse.

Now the married brother also thought to himself: "It is not fair that we divide the grain so evenly. I have many children to care for me in my old age, and my brother has none. I know what I will do! I will take a sack of grain from my storehouse each evening and put it in my brother's storehouse." So each night when it was dark, he likewise carefully carried a sack of grain and put it in his brother's storehouse.

This went on for weeks, and since neither brother knew what the other was doing, each brother was amazed to discover that even though they had removed a sack of grain the night before, they had just as many the following morning.

But one night the brothers stumbled into each other in the darkness halfway between their storehouses, each carrying a sack of grain. It was then that they understood the mystery. They dropped their sacks and embraced each other in tears as they celebrated their love for one another.

Loving others is really nothing more or less than taking the love you have for yourself and transferring that love to others.

Greg worked for a large franchise organization years ago. The nature of his job required that he answer to three different masters: the franchisor, the franchisee system, and the consumer. It was Greg's responsibility to make both the franchisor and franchisee profitable by meeting and satisfying the needs and expectations of consumers. Greg shares how he accomplished this, in large part, through applying the principle of loving others.

Shortly after joining the company I was assigned brand management responsibilities over what was then considered the "red-headed stepchild" to the company's flagship brand, which just happened to sell competing products in the same market category. Although I was excited for the opportunity, I felt some trepidation not knowing how the franchise community would accept a relative newcomer given the somewhat adversarial relationship that already existed between them and the company. Compounding the situation were my own negative feelings toward franchisees, in general, which had grown jaded from previous experiences working in other franchise organizations.

One day it dawned on me that the only hope I would have for success was to gain the trust and confidence of the franchisees. Getting to know the actual people on a personal level seemed like a good place to start.

So I embarked on a self-directed quest to visit as many franchisees as possible to immerse myself in their world. My objectives in doing so were two-fold:

1. I wanted to understand their business from the ground up. Many of the franchisees had been in the system for over twenty years. No one understood the pitfalls for failure and the keys to success better than they did. There was a wealth of knowledge and experience out there that no one from corporate had been willing to listen to and learn from.

2. I believed that if I could develop a personal rapport with the franchisees and gain their trust, I would be seen as a valued partner in their success rather than just another Ivory Tower guy. The obvious benefits of having such a relationship would be greater collaboration and quicker decision making down the road.

I spent nearly a year crisscrossing the country, visiting with franchisees, working in their stores, asking questions, testing new ideas, talking with employees, and getting to know the franchisees (and their families) over countless lunches, dinners, and rounds of golf. I covered thousands of air miles and spent a lot of time in strange hotel rooms away from home during this time, but it was a rewarding experience that eventually delivered positive results.

It wasn't long before I began to develop a genuine love and respect for "my" franchisees. They were not only savvy business operators but great human beings. I discovered that they were just as dedicated and passionate about their business, in fact even more so, as I was about performing my job to the best of my ability. We all genuinely wanted the same thing: what was best for the brand, each other, and the customer. To this day, though I have long since left the company, I have great respect for these franchisees and still consider many of those I met dear friends.

As an indication of the power of the foundational principle we're discussing, before Greg left the company that "red-headed stepchild" was sold at the highest market valuation possible, not only surpassing the flagship brand in sales and profitability but becoming the number-one brand in its market category at the time. Greg attributes much of that success to the mutual trust, respect, and love that was forged between his team and the franchisees.

Henry Ford said, "If there is any one secret of success, it lies in the ability to get the other person's point of view and see things from that person's angle as well as from your own."

The Unified Power Principle of Love comes as a result of applying the "Golden Rule," not the "Rule of Gold." Much about loving others stems from the concept of empathic caring and concern for others.

The noted clinical psychologist Dr. Allen E. Bergin offered a definition for empathy with these two characteristics.

"Empathy is sensitivity to and seeks accurate understanding of a person's feelings, thoughts, experiences, and meanings."

"Empathy is the ability to communicate this sensitivity and understanding to another person."

Carl Rogers, Dr. Bergin's mentor, noted, "Empathy is not a technique but a way of being.... When we are empathic, we are able to enter into the world of another person and feel at home in it without feeling as if we actually are in the other person's world."

By endeavoring to get into the worlds of others by seeking all points of view, showing genuine concern and caring, and providing service to others, you can add a richness of experience and knowledge that will enhance your ability to make better decisions and accomplish more.

Love of God

An inscription scratched on a concentration camp wall read, "I believe in the sun, even when it is not shining. I believe in love, even when feeling it not. I believe in God, even when He is silent."

It may seem odd to bring up the love of God in a discussion on personal and professional productivity. And we do so knowing that the idea of *God* is represented as many different entities and defined differently by so many that it would be foolish of us to narrow the term into a singular identity or description.

For our purposes, the term *God* will refer to the deity, higher power, or influence from which humankind draws strength, guidance, moral direction, or inspiration.

Love of God, figuratively and literally, is encompassed within love of self and love of others. At its core is divine nature and worth, faith in a power higher than self, and selfless acts of kindness.

Because we are all part of the same human race, man's humanity to man is demonstrated by and through the universal language of love.

That's why you will often hear people say or come across the motto, "God is love."

An ancient Chinese proverb teaches us:

I sought my God and my God I could not see.
I sought my soul and my soul eluded me.
I sought to serve my brother in his time of need and found all three:
my God, my soul, and thee.

The love of God, like all other principles of truth, requires action. Love of self and love of others are excellent examples of our love of God in action. Faith that leads to action is another expression of love of God. Whether the challenges are mental, physical, emotional, or spiritual, God does for those who do for themselves. To a large degree, love of God is made apparent when you develop the ability to control events through the use of super faith.

There are three areas in which you can demonstrate love of God: heart, mind, and body.

Your Heart: The greatest of God's work is seen in the changing of one's heart. The love of God can change despair into hope, sorrow into joy, anger into forgiveness, and fear into purpose and action if you are willing to open your heart to the infinite possibilities of His love.

You love God and demonstrate that love by being open to His will or influence, and by surrendering your heart to that love. The nearer you draw to God, the more love you will feel. The more you feel loved, the more open you will be to sharing that love with others and receiving that love from others. This includes understanding and appreciating your own divine worth.

Your Mind: The glory of God is that intelligence which brings meaning and understanding to existence. You show love for God by using your brain and increasing your capacity for thoughtful intent. This includes continuous learning and improvement through both academic and personal study. It involves the pursuit of understanding how divine influences and intelligence are found in the arts, science, philosophy, theology, sociology, government, law, economics, and every other field of study. It includes learning out of the best books and from trusted teachers, mentors, and leaders.

All discovery, invention, insight, and knowledge, whether on a large scale for humankind or merely for personal enlightenment, emanates from the light or spirit of God's love. This power comes to the minds of women and men often through feelings or thoughts. By exerting intellectual power and utilizing all mental faculties at your disposal, and by devoting focused thought through study, contemplation, or prayer, you can gain greater understanding and find new dimensions of meaning to just about anything in life. Most solutions to problems or answers to lifes questions that have any consequence come only after dedicating sufficient time and energy out of one's capacity before the insight that comes from God's love can be accessed.

Your Body: You demonstrate love of God by discovering, developing, and using all of the physical attributes, talents, and gifts you have been blessed with to better yourself and improve the condition of those around you.

This includes taking excellent physical, mental, spiritual, and emotional care of yourself; treating your body and the bodies of others with respect; leading a life of balance between job and family, and work and leisure; dedicating time toward continuous self-improvement and re-charging your internal batteries; and applying knowledge and wisdom in your daily efforts to make a positive impact on the world.

As a synthesis of the importance of love, consider this remarkable account of an individual who exemplified love of self, love of others, and love of God. His name is Douglas Snarr.

When growing up on a small farm in Idaho, Douglas would always sit on the back row of the classroom, hoping beyond hope that he would never be asked to participate in any classroom discussion. The phenomenon of talking was beyond his capability. He was an inveterate stutterer.

As time went on, his stuttering and stammering increased in intensity. He was reduced to writing on a pad when he wanted to communicate. He would even go out of his way to avoid running into people he knew. He avoided all situations requiring speech and channeled his energies, instead, into using his hands for painting signs.

Douglas's love of self suffered as he struggled to maintain a positive mental attitude. He was wrought with fears and anxieties and could find no inner peace with what he viewed as an overwhelming physical handicap. Consequently, he was mentally, emotionally, and spiritually distraught for much of his early life.

One thing he *did* do, though, was to develop his skill at painting. By the time he was a high school senior, he became adept at painting signs and decided to start his own sign company. He would later commit himself to the goal of becoming a millionaire before age thirty, notwithstanding the insurmountable odds that lay ahead, given his speech impediment.

He convinced his boxing partner to join him in his new business. Doug would make the signs and his partner would do all the selling. Their road signs began springing up in and around their hometown. Upon high school graduation Douglas had earned enough money to attend a university. And along the way he had come to recognize that, notwithstanding his physical impediment, he could be of worth to himself and others.

With this new hope, his desire to speak became a passion and then a blinding obsession, until he was consumed day in and day out with a burning need for the gift of speech.

At the university, he enrolled in a class on stuttering, but was shattered when the professor told him that it would be impossible for him to overcome his stuttering. The class, Douglas was told, would simply help him adapt to his impediment.

Late one evening Doug came across a small ad in a magazine that claimed a class in Indianapolis could help people like him overcome stuttering.

Douglas left the university and made his way to Indianapolis where he enrolled in the Benjamin N. Bogue Institute. Douglas was taught the rhythm method of waving his arm while slowly and haltingly saying syllables in a monotone voice. This was encouraging, but after a few weeks at the Institute Douglas began to fail. He said of the experience, "I felt myself sinking deeper and deeper each day as if caught in some indefinable quagmire with no support, grasping frantically for anything, but feeling only the suction that pulled me down, down, down to the very depths of hell." Once again, his love of self was shattered mentally, emotionally, and spiritually.

It was at this point in life that Doug committed to turn to God in a way he had never done before. He always had a deep, abiding love for God and had always said his prayers, and attended church services, but these were more routine than devotion. With heart, mind, and body Douglas fell to his knees and began pleading with God like never before to show him the way and give him the help he so desperately needed. He talked, pleaded, begged. He lost track of time. Finally, when completely exhausted, he felt a spiritual awakening. Douglas said of this experience: "I felt a warm, peaceful reassurance. My spirit had touched a power. I rose with something extra."

It being Sunday Douglas found a nearby church with the hope to attend a meeting. The church was closed. But there was a sign on the door. It had the name and address of an elder in the church.

In a blinding rainstorm Douglas made his way to the home of Wilber Lawrence. With compassion Wilber and his wife, Hope, took this forlorn stranger in for two weeks. They were empathic listeners, expressing a deeply felt understanding of what Doug was going through, and genuine concern for his well being.

A short while later, to Douglas's surprise, he was told that it had been arranged for him to give a short talk in a worship service the following morning using the arm rhythm method he had been taught.

In shock Douglas said, "No, never! I can't do it! I have never done it before!" He was sure he would just stand at the podium, freeze up, and say nothing.

But his benefactors prevailed. Again Douglas prayed with all the faith he could muster for divine power to do the impossible. In Douglas's own words, this is what happened at church the next morning:

I reached the podium, stood firmly, took a deep breath, raised my right arm and began to speak. In that moment I felt a warm, powerful influence attend my presence — a feeling of light and substance. I knew that I could drop my arm, forget the past, and speak out normally, forcefully, as any other man speaks, just as I had always dreamed of doing. Without question, that moment was the most sublime and joyous in my life. The sweetness and ecstasy transcended all that I had ever known before and since, because I could talk.... I testified that God had loosened my tongue.... I choked, I cried, I wept.

That day Douglas returned home victorious. Out of his love for and faith in God, he experienced a change of heart, a change of mind, and a change of a body that experts had told him was impossible to change.

He began expanding his sign company and was well on his way to achieving his million-dollar goal by owning 1,300 large roadside billboard rental signs located in thirteen Western states. Then in 1965 the axe fell.

That year the "Highway Beautification Act" was signed into law by President Lyndon B. Johnson. All roadside billboards were to come down.

Being one to never give up, Douglas went to Washington to lobby Congress to pass his "Snarr Plan" that would not only provide compensation for loss of his signs but for hundreds of other sign companies in the United States. Douglas invested five years and a half million dollars to achieve his goal. In 1970 the Federal Aid Highway Act, which incorporated the Snarr Plan, was passed.

In the years that followed, Douglas pursued a number of business ventures, including becoming the chief executive officer and major stockholder of Positive Thinking Rallies, Inc., where he became one of America's foremost public speakers, participating on the same platform as Paul Harvey, Art Linkletter, Zig Ziglar, Earl Nightingale, and Dr. Norman Vincent Peale. (Adapted from Lee Nelson, *Mormon Fortune Builders,* pp. 1-52.)

Douglas never fails to humbly acknowledge and express his love to those who, over the years, have helped him achieve "the impossible dream." But above all, he freely expresses his love and gratitude to God.

Having been Doug's friend for many years, Charles has seen him grow to superstructure stature while building his life on truths that have stood the test of time, the foremost being love of God, love of others, and love of self.

The Unified Power Principle of Love instills commitment, trust, and confidence in the giver and the receiver. Love, in all its forms, offers greater purpose and meaning to life. It is a binding force that welds together you, others, and God to help create the framework of your superstructure.

Unified Power Steps

1. Practice going to bed and waking up each morning with optimism and eager anticipation for a new day.

2. Change your attitude; change your life.

3. Explore how you can make a more meaningful life, not just make a living.

4. When life gives you lemons, plant an orange tree. Oranges are naturally sweeter.

5. Look for opportunities in every challenge.

6. Pamper yourself at least once a week with something that you love to do.

7. Stop blaming others for your circumstances and start taking personal responsibility.

8. Participate in something bigger than yourself. Donate your time, not just your money, to a charity or person/family in need.

9. Seek inspiration, learning and wisdom in books, people and nature.

10. Commit to spending more quality time with those who matter the most in your life.

11. Find the good in everyone you meet.

12. Give thanks more than you ask.

13. Acknowledge a higher power in all things, and pray daily.

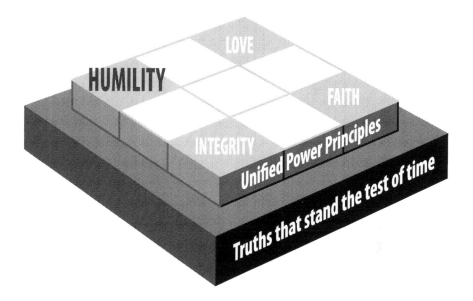

CHAPTER 6

Unified Power Principle #4:
Humility

"It is better to have only a little knowledge combined with humility and small understanding than to possess great treasures of learning combined with foolish self-satisfaction."
— *Author Unknown*

Humility is the quality of being teachable, free from arrogance, void of self-centeredness, slow to anger, unpretentious, and taking no pleasure in superiority. Of the four Unified Power Principles, it is the most misunderstood and the most difficult to master.

Many supposed leaders view humility as antithetical to strength, failing to recognize the true power it can generate in those who possess it. We say "supposed leaders" knowing that at times there are those who may rise to great heights who lack any measure of humility. But if we consider those we would prefer to work for or associate with, we would likely find ourselves drawn to those who exhibit this elusive quality. In fact, throughout history and in our own times, the leaders we admire and remember most—and whose records and accomplishments will stand the test of time—exhibit an abundance of humility.

Benjamin Franklin demonstrated that humility is not only one of the most advantageous virtues one can possess, but also one of the most challenging and elusive to maintain and practice.

Franklin lived the greater part of his eighty-four years striving for balance, harmony, and appropriateness in his life. In his autobiography Franklin describes having botched his younger years so badly that later he saw the need to make amends somehow. He decided the best way to do this was to identify the highest principles he could find, and then to live each and every one of them perfectly for the rest of his life.

He worked on a list of virtues for months before finally settling on twelve: temperance, silence, order, resolution, frugality, industry, sincerity, justice, moderation, cleanliness, tranquility, and chastity.

Satisfied with his list and thinking it complete, he took it to a Quaker friend and solicited his approval.

"What do you think about my list of virtues?" asked Ben.

The Quaker responded, "You need to add one more. Be humble."

Franklin carefully considered his friend's suggestion and then added humility to his list, which we know today as Benjamin Franklin's *Thirteen Virtues.*

Toward the end of his life, Franklin mused how difficult mastering the virtue of humility had been for him. He explained that every time he thought he had achieved humility he would grow proud of his accomplishment and have to start all over again. To this point Golda

Meir, former Prime Minister of Israel, once said: "Don't be so humble. You're not that great."

Several years ago Charles was president of a service organization based in New England and had 200 associates working under his direction. One day Charles received a call informing him that Dr. Robert L. Wood, a man in a high position whom Charles had never met, would be joining him on a three-day tour covering five states. Their time together had such an impact on Charles that he wrote this account of the experience.

When I picked Dr. Wood up at the airport, he approached me with a winning smile and shook my hand enthusiastically as though I was a long-lost friend.

Once in my office he asked me to tell him about myself. After a comment or two about my family he said: "Charles, back up. Let's start with your beginnings. Where did you grow up? Where did you get your education? What have you done professionally?"

Although he had come for the purpose of assessing and advising me on my work performance, for the next fifteen minutes Robert demonstrated the principle of humility and getting into my inner world by focusing all of his attention on me.

I then took the opportunity to ask him to share his personal history with me. Though a little reluctant at first, Bob obliged.

He explained that he was raised in Idaho, earned a doctorate at Harvard University under Dr. Henry Kissinger and other distinguished academics, and later served as department head and dean at the US Naval War College in Rhode Island, as well as Director of Strategic Studies for the Chief of Naval Operations.

After further probing, I learned that when Dr. Kissinger became Secretary of State Bob worked on several key projects related to Kissinger diplomacy. In fact, Dr. Kissinger involved Bob in a key leadership role at the Pentagon. Over the following years Bob worked with chief military officers at the Pentagon under five presidents of the United States.

From that day forward, Bob has been a dear, close friend. He has always been there for me when I needed him. There is nothing we wouldn't do to support each other.

Two things stand out about this remarkable man that are qualities present in all great leaders:

1. He did not promote himself using position or title. He did not voluntarily speak of past or present accomplishments.
2. He possessed the empathic ability to get out of his own world and into the world of others, and to feel at home in both.

In his book *Good to Great,* Jim Collins shares the results of a five-year study of Fortune 500 CEOs. One of the main criteria for the study was identifying CEOs that had achieved and sustained substantial and measurable results over at least a fifteen-year period. Of the 500 CEOs included in the study only eleven ended up meeting the criteria of a great leader.

Through his systematic evaluation of those CEOs who had successfully led their companies to greatness, Collins found that each had "a paradoxical blend of personal humility and professional will. These leaders were self-effacing, quiet, reserved, even shy.... They are more like Lincoln and Socrates than Patton or Caesar." All eleven of the "good to great" CEOs possessed the rare and distinctive quality of humility.

Humility is often characterized by many as a sign of weakness. But nothing could be further from the truth. For when humility is combined with confidence, determination, knowledge, and skills, it is one of the most powerful virtues a person can possess.

There are five predictable characteristics present in a person possessing humility.

1. A turning toward others with concern and compassion.

The humble person possesses kindness, caring, and charity. This person treats everyone with respect and speaks kindly to (and about) all regardless of their position or status. The humble person gives freely of their time and substance, and does so quietly and without any need for recognition.

Greg's father was an educator and highly respected man who worked as a senior administrator for an international institution of higher learning. Greg remembers watching how his father would treat everyone with the same respect and attention, regardless of background or position.

As a young man Greg would often join his father on trips to campuses around the world. He would marvel at how his dad would stop and talk with the grounds crew or painters, remembering each by name and conversing with them about their families and interests, often in their native tongues. In one instant, his father would be speaking to a professor or an administrator about academic matters, and in the next be carrying on a casual conversation with a maintenance worker.

To this day Greg still remembers the names and faces of Mrs. Dean the custodian, Enrique and Miguel the gardeners, Walter the painter, Sam the window washer, and John the grounds keeper.

"Never above, never below, always at eye level." This was the life lesson in humility that Greg learned from his father.

2. An absence of self-adulation.

The humble person always focuses on the positive qualities, strengths, and personal worth of others, instead of elevating himself or herself over them. This person lets actions and reputation speak for themselves. They do not require atta-boys or high-fives to feel their worth or the impact of their contribution.

3. A close connection with reality.

Humility grounds the individual with the realities of who and what they are in relation to others. The humble person always expresses gratitude to others and recognizes his nothingness before a higher power such as God.

"I did it my way" precludes the fact that there is such a thing as divine providence or a helping hand from others along the way. The reality is that no person accomplishes anything in a vacuum.

4. The minimizing of personal accomplishments and possessions in favor of building other people.

A diplomat once had a brief interview with President Abraham Lincoln. As the man left the President's office, a waiting friend asked, "Well, how did it go with Lincoln?" The answer: "He made me feel so good I wondered why I am not President of the United States."

Humble leaders, while at the top of their ladder of success, strive to reach down to pull up others up to the rung on which they are standing. When someone lifts another to the same or higher level, they usually end up with a devoted advocate or loyal life-long friend.

5. An immediate willingness to forgive others who offend.

Webster's dictionary defines forgiveness as overlooking another person's faults and failings.

One of the greatest causes of diminished self-esteem and low productivity happens when a person harbors resentment or jealousy toward another person. Pride, the antithesis of humility, is always at the heart of the problem—and is always what stands in the way of forgiveness.

Pride is being arrogant, angry, self-centered, insubordinate, caught up in self-adulation, putting down others while elevating oneself, and taking pleasure in being at a higher level. Pride consumes positive energy, saps creativity, deters focus, and clouds perspective, objectivity and judgment.

In referring to pride C.S. Lewis wrote:

> *Pride gets no pleasure out of having something, only out of having more of it than the next man.... It is the comparison that makes you proud; the pleasure of being above the rest. Once the element of competition has gone, pride has gone.* (Mere Christianity, *The Macmillan Company Paperback Edition, 1960, p. 95.*)

One of the most frequently quoted verses of scripture is Proverbs 16:18—"Pride goeth before destruction, and a haughty spirit before a fall." And yet so many who seek for power feel immune from the effects of pride. Indeed, our modern landscape is littered with the stories of those who ignore the Unified Power Principle of Humility in their quest to build personal or professional standing.

One such individual rose to tremendous financial, philanthropic, and public heights before learning that he could not ignore his critical need for a foundation built upon the four Unified Power Principles— especially the principle of humility.

Jake came from a pedigreed, east-coast family, one that instilled within him a strong need to succeed, along with a certain sense of entitlement. His family connections helped him gain admission to a respected university that was a bit beyond his abilities, but through a combination of charisma and episodic hard work, he graduated and landed a job with some prestige attached. Even this limited amount of standing was important to Jake, and he soon parlayed it into a series of stepping stones that led to a greater role in the community, a more prominent job, and some notoriety as a public speaker.

While to many what Jake had would have been more than enough, he was motivated by wide-ranging needs—the need to live up to his family's expectations, the need for prominence, and the need for more and more money. Given his mindset, each of these needs seemed to intersect with what some saw as an immense amount of pride.

Using his family's connections, Jake eventually found a commissioned position with a nationally renowned corporation— and soon became a shining star, earning more in just commissions than the company's CEO after his second year. But that was not enough, and soon a scheme hatched to slightly modify the company's proprietary product, falsely claim it as his own, and siphon off a significant portion of the company's customer base. Using his charm, Jake convinced a handful of key employees to take the leap with him and start their own company.

The first few years were rough, as the former company sued and fought to hang onto its intellectual property and customers, eventually winning the case. But by that time Jake's charm and "good" name had already won over an ever-growing customer base, and he was ultimately able to convince any skeptics—and even himself—that the product a court had found him guilty of stealing had actually originated with him. Within a few years, all the allegations and acrimony seemed to vaporize, in part because of the new company's financial success and in part because Jake found countless ways, through his donations, to attach his name to museums, hospital wings, and other high-profile public institutions.

As his wealth went from a few million to tens of millions of dollars, Jake's pride grew as well, taking a marked turn toward uncompromising arrogance. Although he had never possessed much in the way of humility, his burgeoning bank account, his adoring public, and his public persona soon snuffed out what small semblance there had been. And, in the process, he began to feel, in his narcissistic self-love, that he was immune to many of the rules that regulate decent human behavior.

Even with all he had professionally—namely, a company that seemed to just print money—Jake wanted more. In particular, he bristled at the thought of any company or anyone who might upstage him, which led to him launching an ill-advised takeover of his closest competitor. As even casual observers wondered why he would undertake such a costly and risky acquisition, Jake felt impervious to the potential pitfalls.

Around this same time, Jake concluded he deserved more enjoyment in his personal life, despite what seemed to be the ideal marriage and family. So, again feeling above the reach of consequences, he embroiled himself in a series of illicit affairs. At first, he was discrete but, as time went on, he took more and more risks—and after several years of living a double life, his secret life was exposed to full public view, including intense media coverage.

Ultimately, the culture clash created by Jake buying out his closest competitor led to plummeting stock prices and the near disintegration of Jake's once invincible corporation. His shaky leadership and complete lapse in moral and ethical judgment were humility, which eventually resulted in his hand-picked board pursuing every means at its disposal to distance the company from its founder.

Before long, Jake's personal wealth dwindled to scarcely enough to maintain even a semblance of the lifestyle he had once enjoyed. For a time, a few loyal friends helped him with "investments" in what he promised would be his Phoenix rising from the ashes; but before long, no one was left who had any confidence in this once mighty—and mighty proud—man.

There are numerous paths each of us can follow in understanding humility as a cornerstone of our personal superstructure. Jake's path—which led him through the abysses of deception, betrayal, dishonor, arrogance, and contempt for time-honored standards of public and personal decency—is not one to start down. No doubt, his initial steps were taken with a sense of entitlement, a feeling of being protected by his family name, and perhaps a twinge of honest appreciation. But each step he took led him further away from the great principle of humility and toward the destruction that inevitably follows pride.

Humility in no way is a sign of weakness. Rather, it is a sign of inner wisdom and strength, as we view ourselves and treat others based on reality—and not on a distortion or fabrication of our selves and our place in the world.

The Unified Power Principle of Humility, perhaps more than any other power principle, brings balance and appropriateness to one's life. It promotes integrity, rejuvenates faith, and encourages love. A person possessing the virtue of humility will always be able to maintain a superstructure supported by principle and firmly grounded in reality.

Unified Power Steps

1. Never judge others based on appearance or hearsay. And even then, don't judge!

2. When offended, don't harbor a grievance. Let it go.

3. Be empathetic. Actively listen to what others have to say. Take note of their hopes, feelings, and aspirations. Pay attention to them.

4. Learn to love yourself, but don't get too infatuated.

5. Avoid finding fault and pointing out the negative in others; instead, focus on accomplishments and the positive.

6. Delight in the success of others. Build others up every chance you get.

7. Give credit where credit is due.

8. Take satisfaction and joy in your own accomplishments without becoming prideful.

9. Be quick to acknowledge the help of others and a higher power in all your successes.

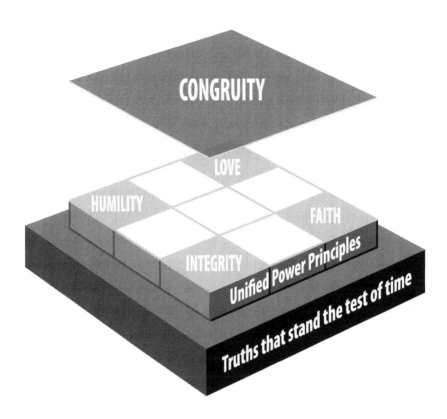

CHAPTER 7

Structural Integration:
Congruity

"Truth that unifies lives is a polished diamond found only at great depths, while at the surface we are constantly unearthing counterfeit broken pieces of glass made up of false traditions."
—*Author Unknown*

With the four Unified Power Principles as your foundational cornerstones, you are ready to explore how integrity, faith, love, and humility can be integrated into the framework of your superstructure to produce Unified Power.

Structural Integration is the process of appropriately and intelligently applying unifying principles to produce balance, harmony, and optimal effect. The world watched an inspiring example of structural integration during the week of August 10, 2008, as Olympian Michael Phelps performed, and achieved, at a level few imagined possible. Indeed, by winning eight gold medals and breaking seven world records, he became the most decorated Olympic medalist in history.

Let's delve into Michael's preparation and execution before and during the Olympics to see how he integrated all four Unified Power Principles.

Integrity

Did he keep all of his commitments? Michael stayed true to himself, his coach, and his teammates by honoring all commitments in and out of the pool, from practice schedules to races to media interviews. He proved trustworthy to his teammates by delivering many of his best performances during his leg of the relay races.

Did he exaggerate the truth? He didn't have to. Michael was expected to win, and in race after race he proved deserving of all the hype and expectations that had been heaped upon him. He did not brag, boast, or trash talk. He just went about his business, race after race, victory after victory. The gold medal podium was the only forum he used to tout his success.

Was he free of any deception? There was no way for Michael to shade his accomplishments or hide deficiencies in a pool of clear water with the entire world watching. In the 100-meter butterfly, the instant replay showed Michael edging out his rival with one last lunge at the wall, winning by just one-hundredth of a second. Under such scrutiny, there could be no arguing or any doubt about outcomes, and Michael gave everything he had in full public view to ensure his success.

Did he lie, steal, or cheat? Michael delivered clean and untainted performances per the IOC's strict testing standards. He prepared for his competitions with no hint of scandal or through unfair advantages.

Was he in close touch with reality? Michael knew what he was capable of and made what seemed impossible possible. As a result of his preparations, Michael was able to confidently say, "If you dream as big as you can dream, anything is possible."

Faith

In every interview, training session, and event leading up to and during the Olympics, Michael consistently exhibited confidence that his worthy goals would be achieved. So how did he do at applying the four Evidences of Faith?

Did he derive full benefit from past achievements that related to his goals? Michael and his coach were not novices when they arrived in Beijing. Michael had already won six gold and two bronze medals at the Athens Olympics in 2004. Entering the 2008 Olympics he was still the world champion and record holder in many of the events he entered.

Leading up to the 2008 Olympics, Michael and his coach mapped out a plan for competing at the National championships, the Pan Pacific championships, and the World championships. Every race at these events was designed to build confidence and to lead Michael to one place—the Olympic podium—by building upon each success one race at a time.

Did he imagine himself performing the necessary steps to achieve his desired result? In his book, *Beneath the Surface,* Michael stated, "When I'm about to fall asleep, I visualize to the point that I know exactly what I want to do: dive, glide, stroke, flip, reach the wall, hit the split time to the hundredth, then swim back again for as many times as I need to finish the race."

On another occasion Michel wrote: "Before the [Olympic] trials I was doing a lot of relaxation exercises and visualization. And I think that that helped me to get a feel of what it was gonna be like when I got there. I knew that I had done everything that I could to get ready for that meet, both physically and mentally."

Did he selectively identify with role models who have achieved greatness? In the sport of swimming, and Olympic swimming in particular, there had always been one "gold" standard since 1974, that being Mark Spitz's seven gold medals at the Munich Olympics.

But by his own admission, Phelps more readily identifies with another superstar in an entirely different sport — basketball. His hero is none other than Michael Jordan, who, like Phelps, is considered by most to be the greatest to ever compete in his sport.

Whether it was the inspiration for greatness he found in Jordan or the storied accomplishments of the legendary Spitz, Michael identified himself with and stood on the shoulders of arguably two of the greatest athletes in history, and emulated their passion and drive to excel at the highest level.

Did he place trust in a higher power other than self? By his own acknowledgment, Michael is not an overly religious man, but he has always maintained a belief in God. Nor has he never backed away from expressions of gratitude to God for blessing him with the body and talent to do what no other man has ever done.

Love

Michael demonstrated an integration of all three categories of love before and during the Olympics.

Love of self: Michael believed in himself and stayed true to his commitment to be the best. He also took excellent care of his mental and physical conditioning to maximize every ounce of talent and potential he had.

Love of others: In spite of having to compete against some of his race relay teammates in individual races, Michael and his teammates demonstrated a deeply felt harmony and respect for each other. Michael explained, "Before we came together as a team, we did not know each other. But when we came into the Olympics, we were of one mind."

Michael also honored the sacrifice and hard work of his mother and coach by living up to his potential, and expressing frequent, ongoing gratitude and appreciation to those who made it possible for him to become the man and athlete he was.

Love of God: By training harder, sacrificing more, practicing longer, and spending more hours in the pool than anyone else to improve his God-given skills and abilities, Michael shared with the world his unique talents in the ultimate display of divine appreciation.

Humility

After arriving in Beijing, Alain Bernard, one of the standout swimmers on the French team and 100-meter world record holder at the time, declared: "The Americans? We will smash them." Michael and his American teammates could have responded with bravado, ego, and trash talk, but they remained humble and silent, and let their actions speak for them.

Later, after the American team set a new world record in the 4x100 relay in one of the preliminary heats, the French team still continued their taunting, including an instance where one of the French swimmers spat in the USA's swim lane during warm-ups.

But Michael and his teammates remained unruffled and humble, choosing to focus their energy and effort on their ultimate goal. When the time came for Michael and his teammates to answer their challengers, they did so in the pool by winning the gold medal in a dramatic come-from-behind victory against none other then the French team.

Michael has openly acknowledged that his incredible feat of eight gold medals at a single Olympics (five individual; three team) would never have been possible without the support of his mother and friends; the help of his long time coach, Bob Bowman; and, most of all, the efforts of his fellow teammates. He gave credit where credit was due.

"Without the help of my teammates this isn't possible," he said. "I was able to be a part of three relays, and we were able to put up a solid team effort and we came together as one unit. The unified team that we had is the difference."

At the 2008 Olympics, Michael became a model of a personal superstructure and Unified Power. To some degree, every individual who strives to achieve worthy goals that are built upon the four Unified Power Principles is an Olympian. How you execute and integrate these principles into your life, however, is the difference between gold, silver, bronze, or not placing.

In addition to all his accomplishments, Michael also proves the point that there has yet to be a human superstructure that is perfect. Despite our best efforts, we all have our flaws and makes mistakes. A few years after the Olympics, Michael was accused of using drugs. He was embarrassed and humiliated and for a short time was banned from racing. But he overcame his mistake, was reinstated, and soon after regained his stature.

The Unified Power Concepts

Structural Integration includes three **Unified Power Concepts** (or **Unified Power Cs**): **Congruity, Competency Plus,** and **Concentration of Power.** Let's begin by examining the first, Congruity.

Congruity is experiencing balance, harmony, and appropriateness with the events in your life.

The Oxford English Dictionary defines *congruity* as harmony of the parts with the whole. It is characterized by conformity with what is right while standing firmly on accepted principles of truth.

To gain a better understanding of congruity, let's return to the example of the Parthenon.

Engineering uses the term *superstructure* to identify that part of a structure that receives the "live load" directly. In a very general sense, live loads are those forces that vary over the life of a structure, but that are continuously supported, maintained, and sustained at maximum capacity and performance.

An example of live load at work is found in the Parthenon's superstructure (that part which is visible and rests on top of the limestone foundation). The superstructure is supported by majestic 8' x 17' pillars set in proportions of four to nine, repeated in different parts of the structure.

The Parthenon's pillars present what are called reduction and tension. *Reduction* refers to the decrease in the pillar's diameter from bottom to top. In contrast, the tension of every pillar is spread throughout its length. This is where the pillar creates its force to keep the weight of the entablature above, which in turn is carried from pillar to pillar. With these architectural innovations, the pillars are able to show not only breadth and movement for aesthetic purposes, but still maintain enough power to support the weight above. In other words, they carry the *live load*.

The pillars, which have a slight inclination toward the inner part of the temple and the entablature above, step on the horizontal, slightly curved lines and support the entire superstructure. Additionally, the corner pillars participate in the inclination of both sides; and, thus, the perfect balance and symmetry of the Parthenon is achieved—a feat countless engineers and individuals have marveled at for centuries!

Webster's Dictionary provides two definitions of a pillar:

1. A slender, freestanding, vertical support.
2. A responsible person of central importance, sometimes referred to as "a pillar of strength."

In a figurative sense, congruity can be represented as the pillars that carry the live load of your superstructure. Congruity helps maintain structural integration by adding strength to sustain form and support the weight of everything that is placed on top of the foundation.

To get a better understanding of how congruity works within the superstructure, it may help to understand what congruity is not.

Incongruity and Disunification

Incongruity is any thought or action that creates imbalance, induces disharmony within oneself and with others, and violates relationships of trust through inappropriate behavior.

The "workaholic" is a perfect example of incongruity at work. This is a person who is 100 percent focused and committed, but is still completely out of balance (and out of touch) with the rest of life. Incongruity happens a lot with people trying to climb the ladder of success, or with those who want and need to appear more important or successful than others. It is not uncommon for these types of individuals to work insane hours while neglecting other important responsibilities and relationships.

Most incongruous (or dysfunctional) behaviors often manifest themselves in dishonesty (lack of integrity), fear (lack of faith), selfishness (lack of love), and pride (lack of humility).

For a moment imagine yourself standing squarely on two feet as you would normally. Your body should feel stabilized and be in complete balance with the ground beneath your feet.

What would happen if you bent your right leg behind you about eight inches off the ground so that you were now standing on just your left foot? Are you a little less balanced? Now what if you shifted your weight up on the ball of your left foot, and then back on the heel of your foot, with your right leg still bent behind you? Would it be difficult to maintain your balance?

People who suffer from incongruities in their life continually struggle to bring their thoughts, relationships, and careers into a state of harmonious equilibrium. As incongruities persist, there is often a tendency to overcompensate or rationalize, which only makes matters worse until self-esteem diminishes and productivity decreases to irrelevant levels.

Think about the impact that incongruous behaviors have on self-esteem and performance in you and others. You've no doubt seen or experienced first-hand how such dysfunction adversely impacts quality of life, fulfillment in relationships, and satisfaction in career. You likely know people who have developed two sets of values and performance standards: one for home and one for work. This is what is called disunification.

Disunification

Disunification occurs within individuals and between individuals. It places the individual at variance with himself and others, and is often the undoing of what could otherwise be unified, harmonious effort. Such dysfunction results to varying degrees in confusion, dissension, discord, alienation, and failure. It wreaks absolute havoc on productivity and teamwork.

One of the greatest causes for incongruity and disunification in people is rationalization. This is how most disunified people seek to legitimize impropriety or justify ineffective action.

When people don't get what they want or get something they don't want, they often use defense mechanisms to blame everyone and everything for their circumstances, especially when they fail to adapt to events that are out of their control. The simple fact is most of the problems that cause lack of balance and harmony are self-inflicted. Disunified people unwisely attempt to reengineer values or modify principles that have stood the test of time in order to fit their dysfunctional, self-serving motives.

The pitfalls of that approach were encapsulated during an exchange Charles once had while presenting a seminar to a group of oil industry executives in Houston, Texas. One of the participants called out, "What if you're ignoring a value that your conscience tells you is true, and you know it is, but you don't want to change?" Charles looked the gentleman straight in the eyes and said, "Suffer!"

As seemingly commonplace as it is, rationalization will never resolve the gap between what you believe to be right and what you know to be of value, and making decisions or performing in a manner that is entirely contrary. Granted, life and decisions may not always be as simple as black and white, or as clear-cut as right and wrong. However, most rationalization occurs when the contrast *is* obvious and the "line" between the two is distinct. It is when you attempt to blur the lines or accept other people's bleeding of boundaries that rationalizing begins to wreak havoc.

Rationalization is like a two-edged sword that is likely to inflict damage no matter which way you swing it. On the one side, the individual uses the blade to protect ego and maintain some semblance of sanity. Many will rationalize a behavior to the point where they see themselves as being dead right when, in fact, they are dead wrong.

The other side of the rationalization blade gives people a false sense of security, resulting in the individual growing increasingly out of touch with reality. People who habitually rationalize do not control events or live by values that bring balance and harmony, but rather use whatever method or means is expedient at the time. While rationalization may appear to help maintain a semblance of temporary harmony for such people, it is ultimately debilitating to self-esteem and productivity because somewhere deep inside us we are aware of the disconnect.

Now that you have a basic understanding of what congruity is and is not, let's turn to one of the most important and powerful elements of Unified Power.

The Doctrine of Self-Unification

Self-unification is the process of aligning one's performance with selected, enduring principles of truth that should be valued most.

Carl Rogers put it this way: "We are in the process of becoming." Congruity between what you should value most and actual performance is achieved through the process of Self-unification. The more you can align your daily performance with unifying principles that have stood the test of time, the better you will feel about yourself, and the more in control of events and productive you will become. High self-esteem is a byproduct of congruity.

To illustrate the concept of Self-unification, try this simple exercise:

Hold your right hand in front of you and make a circle by placing the tip of your thumb on the tip of your index finger. Hold this position as you place your left hand to the immediate left of your right hand, again making a circle with the thumb and index finger.

With the two circles in front of you, select in your mind one of the four Unified Power Principles: integrity, faith, love, or humility.

The circle on your right hand will represent the principle you selected. Because this circle represents an idea of truth that has stood the test of time, it does not move.

The circle on your left hand will represent how congruous your performance has been with the principle you selected over the past two weeks.

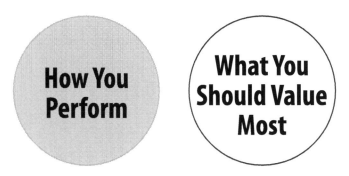

To the extent your actions have been completely incongruous with the selected principle, hold your two hands completely apart. To the extent there has been some disunification but some congruity, move your left hand circle over the right hand circle, creating some overlap.

If your actions have been perfectly in harmony with the principle you selected, bring the left circle exactly over the right circle so that the two form a near perfect union. This oneness represents Unified Power, a self-unified individual possessing high self-esteem and performing with near complete Congruity. (See model on next page)

The doctrine of Self-unification is present with men and women from all walks of life, religions, and value systems. For many people their most important values are derived from religious beliefs and books such as the Bible, Koran, Talmud, or Hindu Vedas. For others, values have been instilled by and learned from parents, teachers, pastors, and peers.

Regardless of the source or extent of your value system, there are certain unalterable truths that have stood the test of time that are common to mankind. For example, each of the four Unified Power Principles are firmly embedded within religion and common law, among other things.

Once you commit to living a life of integrity, faith, love, and humility, and making them the cornerstones of your superstructure, the rewards of Self-unification will become increasingly self-evident.

Ultimately, the goal of developing congruity within your superstructure is to achieve Unified Power by becoming self-unified. Your success will depend, in large part, on your ability to identify those unifying principles you should be valuing most and then actually integrating them into how you live your life, both personal and professional.

Self-Unification

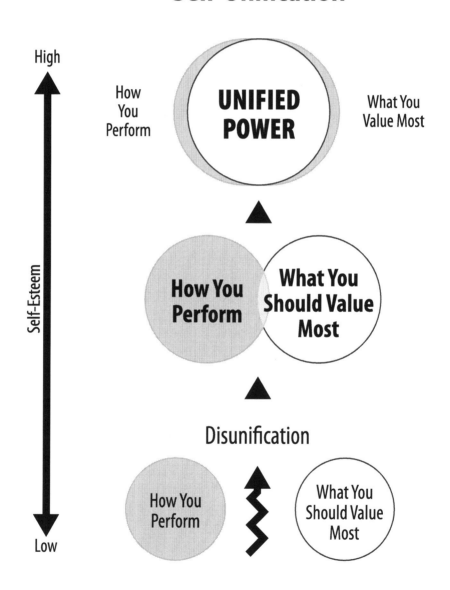

Unified Power Steps

1. Identify at least five values that are important to you and write them down in no particular order of importance. Circle those values that relate to any of the four Unified Power Principles.

2. Using the hand and circle exercise, reflect on your performance over the past two weeks on each of these values. Do your circles overlap, intersect, or not even touch? List specific behaviors, thoughts, or events that reveal any incongruities, and what you plan to do to bring more congruity in your life.

3. Begin today to make a daily, concerted effort to modify your thoughts and actions to reflect your values and bring them into alignment in your daily life. Every time you catch yourself thinking or doing something that is not in harmony with any of the values you identified in step one, make a written note for later evaluation and corrective action.

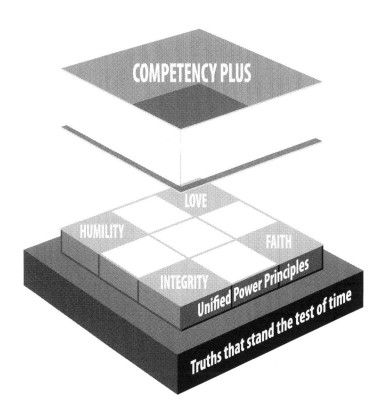

CHAPTER 8

Structural Integration:
Competency Plus

"The idea of excellence comes very near to being the purpose of life itself.... Excellence encourages self-discovery, wakens ambition, arouses industry, inspires emulation, improves every other form of accomplishment. There can be no real success and no real happiness without excellence, and there can be no excellence without effort."

— *Sterling W. Sill*

More than 30 years ago Charles created a company to help individuals and organizations commit to "a higher standard of excellent performance." Today, one of the primary purposes of Unified Power is to raise the bar of performance and productivity even higher by taking a person beyond mere competency to **Competency Plus.**

Webster's Dictionary defines the word *competent* as "being properly qualified, adequate for the stipulated purpose." How does being "properly qualified" or "adequate" produce excellent results? The answer is, it doesn't! Debbi Fields, the founder of Mrs. Fields Cookies, had a motto that she used as a pattern for performance. She called it **GENI: Good Enough Never Is.** Competency is closer to good than it is to better or best. It is closer to average than it is to excellent. Mere competency simply is not good enough when building a Unified Power superstructure that will stand the test of time.

Competency Plus, on the other hand, involves achieving optimal results with a commitment to excellence in accomplishing the most vital priorities through consistent effort and strict accountability. Competency Plus is the schoolmaster of preeminence. Once you have developed a level of Congruity within your superstructure, the application of highly favored skills and relevant knowledge is required to produce optimal results. Whereas Congruity seeks to create a synergistic relationship between belief and behavior, Competency Plus propels individual performance beyond just acceptable, average, or adequate into the stratosphere of stellar and superior.

In the early 1700s a young boy in Italy by the name of Antonio committed himself to the principle of Competency Plus by proclaiming, "I will become the greatest violin maker in the world."

In his late teens, after learning all he could from his mentor Amati (who at the time was one of the most noted of all violin makers), Antonio began creating violins under his own name. At age 21 he wrote in his diary, "Other people will make violins, but no one will make a violin like Antonio Stradivari."

Stradivari soon excelled in every aspect of violin making. He added two inches to his violin when other violins were about the size as a child's violin today. He used special, properly seasoned wood and a unique proprietary formula of varnish. Combining the two (and mixing in his master's touch) resulted in a tonal quality no one in more than 300 years has been able to replicate.

Stradivari built 1,169 string instruments during his lifetime. His creations are still regarded as among the finest stringed instruments ever created. To this day they command millions of dollars from collectors at auctions, and are played as coveted instruments by professional musicians across the world.

Before Antonio died he passed on his skills and special varnish formula to his two sons, who would eventually take their father's violin making secrets to their graves. *"Other people will make violins, but no one will make a violin like Antonio Stradivari."*

What gave Antonio Stradivari the ability to achieve such accomplishments that have endured and increased in value over centuries? The answer is found in his moving beyond "basic qualifications" and "acceptable work product" toward Competency Plus. By securing additional knowledge and training at the highest levels from role models who had already achieved greatness, and by developing and increasing his skill level through self-discovery, practice and continuous innovation, Antonio held himself personally accountable to a higher standard of achievement. His every thought and action reflected an undeviating drive toward excellence by carrying out his most vital priorities.

So, how do the rest of us get from mere competency to Competency Plus? Consider the following examples and steps for attaining optimal (and quality) productivity:

1. Stand on the shoulders of giants.

A "giant" is someone who has excelled beyond the ordinary. Such a person oft times is viewed as being "larger than life" or a "pillar of strength." These individuals represent superstructures built upon Congruity at the highest level.

"By almost universal agreement Isaac Newton was the greatest scientist who has ever lived." (*In the Presence of the Creator: Isaac Newton and His Times,* Gale E. Christianson [Norwalk, Connecticut: The Eastern Press, 1984], p. vii.)

He discovered how the universe was held together through his theory of gravity. He made significant contributions to mathematics, physics, and astronomy. He gave us calculus and groundbreaking discoveries on light and color.

Throughout his life Isaac Newton sought and associated with some of the greatest thinkers of his day including Edmund Hailey, Gottfried Wilhelm Leibnitz, Robert Hooke, Sir Thomas Wren, and John Locke, all giants in their fields of study.

Later in life, with congruous humility, Sir Isaac Newton said of himself, "I do not know what I may appear to the world, but to myself I seem to have been only like a boy playing on the seashore, and diverting myself now and then finding a smoother pebble or a prettier shell than ordinary, whilst the great ocean of truth lay all undiscovered before me." At another time when he was being honored for his accomplishments he said, "If I have seen further, it is only that I have stood on the shoulders of giants."

In his great book, *Think and Grow Rich*, Napoleon Hill introduces a similar concept to that of standing on the shoulders of giants in what he called a "Master Mind" group. He defined the purpose of this group as the "Coordination of knowledge and effort in a spirit of harmony, between two or more people, for the attainment of a definite purpose."

By carefully selecting individuals who you can trust to serve as mentors or teachers, you can leverage human capital in the form of collective experience and knowledge from those who have already excelled. These so-called "giants" or "master minds" will help you define your purpose, sharpen your focus, improve your plan, and stay committed until you have accomplished your high-value goals and achieved optimal productivity.

Almost without exception, high achievers have always found their way to successful endeavors by following the same pattern as Sir Isaac Newton and others. Stradivari stood on the shoulders of Amati. Plato stood on the shoulders of Socrates. Aristotle stood on the shoulders of Plato. Alexander the Great stood on the shoulders of Aristotle. These superstructures, and countless others like them, have all stood on the "shoulders of giants."

2. Engage in continuous learning with a focus on the most vital priorities.

"No man ever reached to excellence in any one act or profession without having passed through the slow and painful process of study and preparation." (Quintus Horatius Flaccus, renowned Roman poet, first century B.C.)

The process of continuous learning and acquisition of knowledge develops intellectual insights and understanding that tap into the infinite capacity of the human mind. By seeking, obtaining, and organizing knowledge and experience, either through one's own efforts or through the sharing of ideas with others, a person gains greater assurance that worthy aspirations and desired results can be achieved.

Formal education and advanced degrees, while important contributing factors, are not the final answer. Thomas Edison only had three months of formal schooling, and Henry Ford only a sixth grade education. In his early years Douglas Snarr had such a severe handicap with stuttering that the only way he could communicate was to write what he had to say on a piece of paper. Scholastic limitations did not stop these men from seeking knowledge through continuous self-study and inquiry. Instead, each learned how to leverage the principles of knowledge and convert them into action until they achieved their desired outcomes. Every failure and naysayer, every obstacle and challenge, only brought them closer to success.

Abraham Lincoln, though he received only four months of formal schooling, used to walk to school with his sister through nine miles of animal-infested timberland. His early boyhood readings were primarily the family Bible and Aesop's Fables. As a boy he had such a thirst for knowledge he would walk miles just to borrow a book to read.

Abe once said to a friend, "The things I want to know are in books. My best friend is a man who will git me a book I ain't read." Abe even carried a book with him when plowing a field. He would read at the end of a furrow while resting the horses. Sometimes he even rested the book between the handles while he plowed. (Carl Sandburg, *Abraham Lincoln* [New York: Charles Scribner's Sons, 1950], vol. 1, p. 3.)

"Lincoln was committed to studious habits, greed for information, a thorough mastery of the difficulties of every new position in which he was placed." (*Ibid.*, 30.)

3. Transform knowledge into skills and action.

Sir Francis Bacon had it only half right when he said, "Knowledge is power." (*Religious Meditations: Of Heresies,* 1597.) Knowledge on its own does not generate action, productivity, or superior performance. By itself, knowledge is only unapplied intelligence that produces little or no results.

Real power, the kind that leads to achievement, can only be secured through the application of knowledge directed toward intended outcomes. Learning just for the sake of knowledge does not build Competency Plus unless what is learned is organized with purpose and focus, and focused on clearly defined outcomes. If only more colleges and universities took this approach in preparing students for a more productive life in the future, far more graduates would attain greater and deeper levels of success, contribution and fulfillment out of life.

In the many biographies of great achievers, one of the common threads running through each person's life was an insatiable appetite for acquiring knowledge and applying it in pursuit of achievement. All great achievers come to the realization that it is not what you know, but what you do with what you know that makes the difference between success and failure, average and great, competent and Competency Plus.

Unified Power Steps

1. Identify at least two or three "giants" that can be part of your "master mind" group. These individuals will become your mentors, coaches, and greatest advocates. Arrange a meeting to share your unifying principles and high-value goals with them. This process will commit you to greater action.

2. Select at least six biographies of past or present achievers to read within the next year. As you read, highlight significant passages and key takeaways (action items) from each book, including making notes to yourself in the margins.

3. After reading each book, review the highlighted portions and personal notations, and create an action plan for incorporating them into your thought process and performance expectations. Refer back to these books and your notes from time to time to inspire and direct your activities.

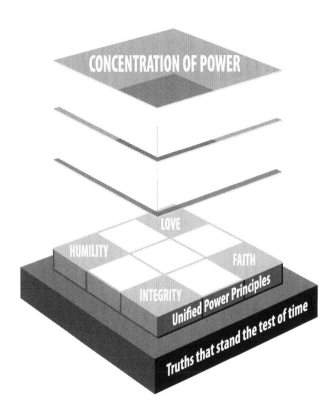

CHAPTER 9

Structural Integration:
Concentration of Power

"Whatever you can do, or dream you can, begin it. Boldness has genius, power and magic in it."

—*Goethe*

Now that you understand how Congruity and Competency Plus work together to add greater power to your personal superstructure, it is time to introduce the third Unified Power Concept of Structural Integration, Concentration of Power.

Concentration in its most basic form means to focus upon. Power is defined as the ability to produce effect. Therefore, **Concentration of Power is the ability to focus upon and accomplish the most vital priorities and thereby produce optimal effect.**

All thought leads to some form of action—positive or negative, productive or destructive. When thoughts are transformed into concerted and directed action, especially those backed by a purpose and plan based on unifying principles, they generate the power needed to produce desired results.

The ability to systematically and relentlessly focus on your most valued priorities in a way that maximizes quality productivity and leads to desired outcomes is the result of Concentration of Power.

Charles's account of how the concept of Concentration of Power came to be provides a blueprint that will yield tremendous results in your own life:

One morning in the early development of Time Power, I sat musing over the question, "How can an individual optimize his or her personal productivity?" In my search for an answer I turned to Ralph Waldo Emerson's Essay on History and read, ". . . there is properly no history, only biography. Every mind must know the whole lesson for itself — must go over the whole ground."

It struck me like a bolt of lightning: I will find the answer to my question in the biographies of men and women who have optimized their personal productivity. I will learn for myself the lessons they learned. As far as possible I will explore "the whole ground."

Over the months that followed I read no fewer than fifty biographies, systematically studying the lives of successful industrialists, composers, artists, scientists, statesmen, religious leaders, and influential teachers. I searched for common threads that ran through how these high producers achieved eminent results.

It wasn't long before I observed four common characteristics in all great achievers:

1. *Each had ability to identify the most vital priorities that would make a difference in their occupation or endeavor.*
2. *Each left no stone unturned in acquiring essential knowledge and skills to accomplish their goals through preparation, study and action.*
3. *Each was self-reliant and held fast to their own convictions. They did not let what other people thought or said distract them from their pursuit. In his essay on self-reliance Ralph Waldo Emerson wrote, "It is only as a man puts off all foreign support, and stands alone, that I see him to be strong and prevail."*
4. *Each tirelessly maintained an undeviating course of action until their vision, mission and goals were accomplished, often against great odds.*

Florence Nightingale was just such an example of Concentration of Power in action. For at least seventy of her ninety years, this remarkable English woman struggled and fought against tradition and ignorance, with a singular focus on hospital reform. She studied all she could find on what the leaders in health care and science of the day had to offer. She eventually became one of the world's eminent authorities on scientific care of the sick, organized the first school of nursing in England, and is considered the founder of the modern nursing profession. Countless advances that have grown out of her work in the years since confirm that she was one of the greatest women of England's Victorian Age.

Nikola Tesla is another example of someone possessing an acutely high level of Concentration of Power. Biographer Margaret Cheney noted that he "was possibly the greatest inventor that ever lived."

Tesla gave us the electric motor, alternating current, and radio waves. As the master of electricity, he built a generator that transmitted electricity for thousands of miles on a wire. By contrast, Thomas Edison's generator could transmit electricity only a half mile. Tesla introduced the fundamentals of robotics, computers, missile science, microwaves, beam weapons, and nuclear fusion.

Early in his career, Tesla worked for Thomas Edison, but only for two weeks. They clashed over their differing approaches to scientific inquiry. Edison was a "trial and error" man with the ability to delegate projects to other great inventive minds like Charles Bachelor and Frances Upland. Tesla was more of a loner, preferring to trust in his own judgment and methods of inquiry. Some biographers have said that the greatest mistake Thomas Edison ever made in his life was letting Tesla go.

Tesla would later sell a patent to George Westinghouse with the commitment that he would receive a royalty for every watt Westinghouse transmitted using his electric current. The Westinghouse Corporation later found it could not afford to honor the contract, and convinced Tesla to sell the rights to his electric current for a mere one million dollars. If the original contract had held, Tesla would have become the wealthiest man in the world.

Though he differed from Tesla in many ways, Edison also had a remarkable ability to concentrate his faculties and talents on generating power. He gave the world 1,100 inventions, including the incandescent light, phonograph, mimeograph machine, stock ticker, telephone transmitter, and motion pictures. Edison had the ability to focus upon and accomplish his most vital priorities in producing optimal effect. One evidence of his remarkable skills was his ability to turn every failure from a defeat into a course of action toward success.

Ludwig van Beethoven was one of the greatest composers of all time. His most influential mentors were Hayden and Mozart. Beethoven developed his own distinctive style, which culminated in his glorious Ninth Symphony. To this day many creative pieces of music have been composed, drawing, in large part, from Beethoven's genius ability to focus his skills and talents to produce masterpieces that have stood the test of time.

Countless examples can be found in our own day as well. Early in his career Greg worked with a man who demonstrated many of the qualities and attributes consistent with being a superstructure. A successful sales professional, a loyal friend, a dedicated family man, and just a wonderful human being, it seemed as if there was no aspect of Joe's life that wasn't unified and in harmony.

Joe possessed the rare combination of setting lofty goals based on what he valued most and then stopping at nothing until he achieved them. Joe was driven to excel, but what made him all the more special was that his drive wasn't just about him. In fact, he derived as much satisfaction from helping his colleagues and customers accomplish their goals as he did in achieving those he set for himself.

Added to those qualities was a remarkable degree of humility. Even though, by any measure, Joe had much to be proud of, he never sought special attention for his accomplishments, nor did ever try to elevate himself above his peers. Finally, Joe always maintained professional and personal integrity, he demonstrated a genuine concern for others that was usually backed up by a helping hand or an encouraging word, and he had unfailing faith in his God-given abilities. Taken as a whole, Joe had built a unique and unified superstructure in both his professional and personal life.

Joe was usually the first to arrive at work in the morning and the last to leave. He was the first to volunteer. He was the first to celebrate others' success. He was never profane, nor did he ever demean anyone or complain about a difficult client—or even the weather! Joe simply went about his work in a positive, value-based, and purpose-driven manner, even as he continually stretched himself to do things he had never done before. In many ways, Joe's ability to focus on directed effort enabled him and his associates to surpass previous accomplishments and raise the bar even higher.

Sometimes Joe's commitment to achieving excellence included some rather unorthodox approaches, such as the time he ended up participating in the annual Swim to Alcatraz Race in San Francisco.

At a critical juncture, our company had developed a new computer platform Joe was helping to launch. As part of his effort, Joe challenged the team to meet a rather lofty sales quota of selling fifty units in a relatively short period of time. Knowing that this was no easy task, Joe added additional motivation by telling his team that if they didn't meet their quota, he would swim in the race to Alcatraz, a gut-wrenching 1.5-mile race in frigid 54-degree, shark-invested waters that took place in the strong currents between San Francisco and the former federal penitentiary commonly known as "The Rock."

Joe's belief was that his colleagues would do everything they could to keep him from having to make this swim. But he also knew that he had to lead by example, so he worked in every way he could to help the team meet the goal. Although his sales associates did their level best, by the end of the promotional window only eighteen out of the fifty units had been sold. Of the eighteen, the man Greg had affectionately dubbed "the Sales Guru" was responsible for 15. Given his contribution, it would have been easy for Joe to make excuses, blame others, and renege on his commitment; but he had made a commitment he intended to honor, and he continued his preparations to swim in the race.

The rigors of this race are even daunting for most elite athletes, and Joe really wasn't a big-time athlete or even a serious swimmer. For that matter, he was barely a recreational swimmer. But over the course of eight months, Joe trained before work, during lunch breaks, and after work. He had carefully constructed a workout plan and daily regimen consisting of physical training and proper eating, coupled with healthy doses of positive attitude. And, in typical Joe fashion, he brought the entire office and even his customers along for the ride in his quest to do the unthinkable. It wasn't long before the entire community was talking about Joe and his Alcatraz swim. People rallied to support Joe in his goal with moral support and encouragement. Because he dared to dream and act big, everyone who knew Joe or about his story was brought into his world as if they would be swimming alongside him.

The day finally came for Joe to swim the race. He was well prepared, both physically and mentally. And at his side were his boss, sales colleagues, and other executives from the company—all of whom had made an 800-mile roundtrip to lend their support and cheered him on.

Joe didn't set any records that day. In fact, he finished the race near the back of the pack—and was actually beaten by a dog! Nonetheless, Joe became a rock star, both within the company and his community. Not because of the inspiration people gained from his efforts. And not because he successfully survived the treacherous waters that surround Alcatraz. For as significant as those accomplishments were, they were merely external evidences of the fact that Joe had built his professional and personal life on a rock-solid foundation of integrity, faith, love and humility. In accomplishing his goals, including completing the Alcatraz race, he demonstrated Congruity, Competency Plus, and Concentration of Power.

All great achievers possess the unique ability to focus on their most valued priorities, coupled with a determination and passion to produce results from them. But Concentration of Power leading to great achievement does not apply only to the renowned and pre-eminent. This trait can be brought to bear in the lives of just about anyone in any situation, including you.

A reporter once asked Ida Tarbel, who has written biographies on such notables as Abraham Lincoln, "Of all the illustrious people you know of, who would you say are the greatest?" She replied, "Those people no one knows anything about."

Not everyone can be a Nightingale, Tesla, Edison, or Beethoven; but every human being is endowed with a gift, talent or ability to deliver meaningful results if nurtured and applied correctly. What is your gift? What have you done to develop it? How have you used it to benefit your life or the lives of others? The ability to develop your gift, direct your thoughts, plan your actions, and then focus on the things you value most to produce results is the difference between achievement and stagnation. Through Concentration of Power you can begin to bring certain anticipated events into control; some which may currently seem beyond your wildest imagination. That must not stop you. Dare to dream. Act to achieve.

Will Durant, who wrote the acclaimed ten-volume *The History of Civilization,* said, "History is events of the past." So, you look at your own history. You look at other people's history. You examine the positive and negative consequences of what you've done and what they did.

From such exploration your knowledge expands. You come to understand that selective events from the past can empower you to anticipate events in the future, especially those you bring under control. With renewed confidence you commit to a course of preparation, planning, and the setting of goals, followed by the relentless application of your knowledge and gifts to accomplish your most vital priorities. And then you never lose focus and you never give up until the desired outcome has been achieved. This is the key to all great advancement and achievement.

In 1892 the great psychologist William James set forth four rules for changing behavior.* These rules provide a roadmap for attaining and maintaining Concentration of Power in your life.

Rule 1: Seize the first opportunity to act on the new resolution.

Waiting for the right time is the biggest mistake most people make. Why? Because it will never come. Procrastination in planning will undercut the best of intentions. Start right now while your desire is strong. Write down thoughts and ideas that pertain to your unifying principles and high-value goals as soon as they enter your mind. After you've written them down, move with decisive action at the very first opportunity to apply them in your life.

One of the most critical commitments you will make in developing Unified Power will fall within twenty-four hours of reading this book. Upon completion, you should commit to spending at least five hours of uninterrupted time for self-discovery and for planning how to build your superstructure by integrating the Unified Power Principles and the 3 Power C's (Unified Power Concepts) into your life. Within those five hours you will develop a working blueprint for your superstructure that will set you on an immediate course of action.

One of Charles' former clients, a senior manager of a large corporation, seized on his first opportunity and headed straight for a beach some 600 miles away. There he spent not just the recommended five hours but the next three days formulating his unifying principles and creating his life and company goals for what would later become a superstructure that far exceeded his expectations. This individual became a giant and a pillar of strength to thousands under his influence.

Rule 2: Launch yourself with the strongest possible initiative.

W. H. Murray explained:

Until one is committed there is hesitancy, the chance to draw back, always ineffectiveness. Concerning all acts of initiative (and creation) there is one elementary truth, the ignorance of which kills countless ideas and splendid plans: that the moment one definitely commits oneself, then providence moves too.

All sorts of things occur to help one that would never otherwise have occurred. A whole stream of events issues from the decision, raising in one's favor all manner of unforeseen incidents and meetings and material assistance which no mind could have dreamt would have come his way.

Your upward linear drive toward a Unified Power superstructure can only begin when you start the process with bold audacity. Formulate your unifying principles with a sense of vital urgency as if the rest of your life depended on it, because to a large degree it does. Do not hesitate. Do not deviate. Act now!

Rule 3: Keep the faculty of effort alive with daily practice.

Is it really possible for significant change to take place in your personal and professional life after developing unifying principles and aligning your goals with them?

When Charles was a doctoral student at Columbia University, he often raised a similar question with colleagues and professors. He wondered how all the training and instruction he was receiving could really change his life and the lives of others. Since then one of Charles's missions in life has been to positively affect the lives of as many people as he can through meaningful training and continuous follow-up. Early in his career Charles wrote the following indispensable goal that he has kept front and center in his daily planner for decades:

I have my direction. I will not hesitate. I will not deviate. I will not capitulate, and I will be heard.

Charles's life and career have validated his hypothesis that the right training and knowledge, if supported by daily follow-up and concerted effort, can bring about significant and meaningful change in people's lives. He still receives calls from clients from as far back as thirty years ago who are living by their unifying principles and achieving their goals each day.

Rule 4: Never suffer an exception to occur until the habit is securely rooted in your life.

On November 22, 1975, Charles wrote his first set of unifying principles. In his daily planning, Charles made a commitment to himself that he would visualize and realize the achievement of at least one unifying principle every day until the day he died without exception. Charles wrote the following goal:

This day and every day for the rest of my life I will have a period of solitude for the purpose of applying positive affirmations of faith in the attainment of my worthy goals.

To this day Charles has been faithful in keeping this commitment, with one exception. In 1994 he became deathly ill. There are several blank pages in his daily plenner during this period when Charles was unable to write. Other than this one exception, Charles has prioritized a Daily Action List during a period of solitude planning each and every day, drawing upon his unifying principles.

Concentration of Power is not a secret formula or magic key for success. All great achievers, past and present, have accomplished incredible success and made unimaginable advancements by focusing on their most vital priorities with an undaunted passion to achieve their objectives. This same power to excel and achieve lies within every human being, and is within your reach.

By modeling high achievers and applying James's four rules for changing behavior in your life, you can become a highly productive achiever.

Unified Power Steps*

1. **Seize the first opportunity to act NOW!**
   As soon as you finish reading this book take a minimum of five hours to create a plan of action for yourself. (Chapter 11 will give you more guidelines on how this is to be done.) Review and revise this plan at least once a year.

2. **Launch yourself with the strongest possible initiative.**
   After writing and prioritizing your unifying principles and your most vital goals, share them with at least one other person you trust. This person will provide much needed feedback and support in helping to get you started and stay committed.

3. **Keep the faculty of effort alive with daily practice.**
   Take at least fifteen-thirty minutes every day for a period of

solitude planning. Use this time to review, write, and prioritize your most vital goals as part of a daily action list.

4. **Never suffer an exception to occur.**
   Commit now, and recommit every day during your planning sessions, to *never* let a day pass where you fail to review your unifying principles and chart a course for daily action based on what you should be valuing most.

*Adapted from William James's four rules of habit in *The Principles of Psychology*, New York: Henry Holt, 1890.

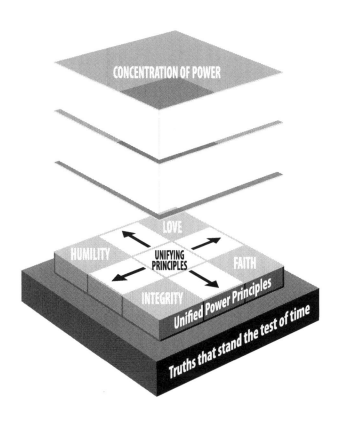

CHAPTER 10

The Unified Power Process:
Identifying, Integrating, and Aligning Your Unifying Principles

"Nothing can bring you peace but yourself in the triumph of principles."

— *Ralph Waldo Emerson (Essay on Self-Reliance)*

When Charles began adapting the concepts of Ben Franklin into his development of unifying principles, he asked himself: "What literature do I turn to in finding truths that have stood the test of time?" Interestingly, decades before, Charles had engaged in a study of the enduring world religions and was impressed to learn that all contained some form of the Golden Rule—that we do to others as we would want them to do to us. This realization, together with other inspired principles, has reinforced Charles's belief that all enduring truth can be circumscribed into one unified whole.

Over the years Charles has also drawn from other sources such as Shakespeare, Socrates, Plato, Aristotle, Emerson, and many others. He enjoyed reading the philosophers and gleaning what he could from them, but has always maintained that timeless religious works are far more substantial sources to draw upon when securing enduring truths. The principles of integrity, faith, love, and humility are expounded in nearly all religious works, reinforcing their rightful place as the four foundational cornerstones to any personal superstructure.

Without question there are many additional unifying principles that will add power to any personal superstructure. As you selectively identify, formulate, and integrate these additional unifying principles into your superstructure, self-unification can be even more securely achieved in your life.

So how do you identify these other principles? Where do you find them? Like most pursuits of any real consequence, the process of identifying, prioritizing, and aligning your performance with what matters most is not always easy. But nothing of any lasting value ever is, and you must be willing to pay the price in honest introspection and endeavor. To illustrate this process, let's take a look into the world of gymnastics.

The balance beam or "beam" used in female gymnastics is a long, narrow apparatus that is 4.1 feet high, 16.4 feet long, and just 4 inches wide. Skilled gymnasts are able to do incredible dance and acrobatic maneuvers on this narrow beam that would seem impossible for the rest of us.

Pretend for a moment that you are now standing on top of one end of the beam. A person on the other end calls out to you saying, "If you will walk across the beam within five seconds, I will give you a one-hundred dollar bill!" Your mind starts computing the difference between two values: personal safety and financial gain. After a quick assessment, many of you would attempt to cross the beam because the value placed on your personal safety in this case is not substantially at odds with the value you place on money.

Now let's look at these same two values in an entirely different context.

In a remote wilderness area several miles southwest of Capital Reef National Monument in Southern Utah, a road winds from the small town of Escalante to the town of Boulder.

Many years ago Charles and his wife, Nola, decided to drive this scenic route on what was then a rocky dirt road. After driving just a few miles, they found themselves traveling on the ridge of a steep mountain the locals called Hog's Back. The mountain dropped off steeply for a few hundred feet on both sides, with the road only wide enough for one car in most places.

In spite of some nervous moments along the way, the two finally arrived safely in Boulder and enjoyed a wonderful picnic in this secluded paradise. As they were about to make the return trip, a local rancher pulled up and suggested they take a different route back called Hell's Backbone. Charles responded with, "I thought that's where we just came from."

The rancher laughed, and then went on to explain that Hell's Backbone was once a natural rock bridge that spanned a 1,000-foot chasm. Unfortunately, a few years earlier, some 120 feet of the rock had dislodged, making the natural bridge route impassable. However, the rancher described how a narrow manmade bridge had since been installed that could be used to safely cross the chasm. The rancher assured the two that the scenery on this return route would be well worth it. Deciding to continue their adventure, Charles and Nola traversed the chasm and enjoyed a scenic drive not experienced by most.

Hypothetically, imagine you are standing on edge of the chasm at Hell's Backbone. The bridge is yet to be built. A helicopter hovers overhead, hauling a super-sized balance beam 120 feet long and 4 inches wide. It positions the beam across the chasm until it is securely positioned on both sides.

The same person as before now invites you to walk across it for the same one-hundred dollar bill offered when the balance beam was just

16.4 feet long and just 4.1 feet off the ground. Does your brain need very long to compute the competing values this time? No way, right? But what if the person offered one thousand dollars? Or one million dollars?

Unless you are a little insane or come from an extremely talented family of Russian gymnasts, no amount of money is likely to persuade you to cross that beam. Why? Because, in this case, the value you place on your life trumps the value you place on financial gain.

Now let's take this analogy a step further. Pretend there is now a really rough looking character standing on the other side of the chasm, and that he is holding one of your children over the edge of the chasm. He yells out, "If you don't walk across this beam in the next sixty seconds, I'm going to drop this kid." Do you walk across the beam or not?

One time Charles asked this question after telling a similar story when a man yelled out, "It depends on which kid!"

In another seminar a woman jumped to her feet during a similar example, and ran sobbing out of the room. A short while later, during a break, she returned and shared the following story with Charles:

Seven years ago I was watering my front lawn while keeping a close eye on my three-year-old daughter playing at the curb. Suddenly, I saw a runaway car speeding down the hill, with no driver, heading straight for my daughter. Frantic, I threw myself in front of the speeding car while hoping to thrust her out of harm's way. She was killed instantly. Seriously injured, I was hospitalized for several months. Ever since that accident, seven years ago, I have not been able to speak one word to anyone of the incident...until now.

Charles felt horrible for causing her distress and started to apologize when the woman grabbed him by the arm and, with tears flowing, looked him straight in the eyes, saying: "You don't need to apologize. I am here to thank you! I now feel free of the heavy burden I have been carrying all these years."

This woman saw herself as a self-unified person for the first time in her life. She had spontaneously attempted to sacrifice her own life for what she valued most, her precious little girl. She finally realized that her life was in harmony with one of her highest priorities. She had come to see the reality of her personal worth. Her values and her performance were completely congruous.

There always has to be an underlying motive or value placed before any action can take place. Just as you wouldn't walk across the beam for a million dollars, yet for no money and at tremendous personal risk, you would cross for your child. In this scenario, the unifying principle of "loving your child" would supersede your other unifying principle of self-preservation.

Everyone makes decisions based on values they determine to be of higher or lesser importance. This can be viewed as an expression of congruity between what is valued most and actual performance. As mentioned earlier, a unifying principle is an idea of truth used as a guide in goal planning and living. It is not simply what you value most, but, more important, what you *should* be valuing most.

The following seven-step Unified Power identification process is designed to help you select your most important unifying principles (in addition to the foundational four: integrity, faith, love, and humility).

Step 1: Make sure your unifying principles represent the highest ideals and truth, and are mutually compatible with each other.

Keep in mind that a principle that is among the highest forms of truth is an idea that has stood the scrutiny and test of time. As mentioned earlier, a good place to find these types of truths is in religious works or in the writings of great thinkers, authors, and poets. Let your heart and your conscience, not how you have been conditioned to think by others or what the world portrays as important, determine what you identify as *your* most important unifying principles.

Remember, for you to become self-unified in a way that endures, you cannot live a double standard. You may be able to fool others some of the time, but you can never fool yourself in the end. No matter how hard you try to conceal your true motives or rationalize your thoughts and behavior, "the real you" will eventually surface in relationships and performance. It does not work to abide by one set of rules or values weekdays at work, and by a different set of values weeknights and weekends at home or elsewhere. When your thoughts and actions conflict, there can be no true Congruity, Competency Plus, or Concentration of Power.

A man once proclaimed to his friend, "I'm going to become wealthy at any cost." Would you put that down as a unifying principle? Would you make such a commitment? Why not? For starters, such a goal would likely be incompatible with other unifying principles, and ultimately prove to have too high a cost in relation to them. That was certainly true for this man. He married well, had a couple of children, started a successful business, and was making good money. But still this wasn't enough. Rationalization set in and he ended up in prison for extortion and fraud. Subsequently, his family left him, and he killed himself. This is an extreme example, but you get the point.

In other cases, you may need to look more deeply at the principles you've selected. During a follow-up session after a seminar, one participant said to Charles, "There's no way I can make two of my unifying principles fit. It looks to me like you can't have a complete set of unifying principles that mesh together."

When Charles asked the gentleman which two principles he was referring to, he answered, "Self-esteem and humility."

Let's look at the definitions of self-esteem and humility again to see if they are mutually compatible. Self-esteem is having a strong sense of personal worth as you relate to yourself and others. Humility is being teachable, free from arrogance, void of self-centeredness, slow to anger, unpretentious, and not taking pleasure in being above others.

It turns out that this man was confusing self-esteem with egotism. If an individual defines self-esteem as egotism, and has humility as another unifying principle, these two unifying principles would, indeed, be incompatible.

After considering these definitions and the behaviors associated with them, the man discovered that self-esteem and humility were not only compatible, but when applied correctly had the potential to generate awesome personal power.

Step 2: Write down those values or principles you should value most.

Include at the top of the list integrity, faith, love, and humility. Then ask yourself the following question:

If I could choose only six to eight unifying principles to guide my future performance, which ones would I choose?

During this process, you may end up choosing unifying principles relating to leadership, service, excellence, success, or respect.

While developing your list, think of incongruities in your current behavior and then add specific principles to your list that, when lived, will help guide you out of these dysfunctional behaviors. Another question to ask yourself might be: "What other qualities or attributes do I need to cultivate in order to bring more balance, harmony, and personal fulfillment into my world?

Step 3: Write each valued priority in your list as an action statement.

By simply adding a verb to each principle selected in step 1, you will convert them into an action statement for an anticipated behavior you seek to control.

Your reformulated list might look something like this:

- Demonstrate impeccable integrity.
- Exercise super faith.
- Love my family.
- Be humble.
- Display effective leadership skills.
- Go the second mile in serving others.
- Commit to excellence in everything I do.

Step 4: Write a paragraph of clarification under each unifying principle.

The simplest way to do this is to take your action statements written in step 3 and write each on top of a separate sheet of paper. Underneath each statement, leave enough space to write one or two short paragraphs of no more than three to four sentences clarifying each unifying principle.

Feel free to use a dictionary or research the Internet and other sources to help you clarify, define, and refine your clarification of each unifying principle.

Here are three examples:

Love my family. I will build a close relationship with my spouse and children, showing care, respect, and kindness to them every day. I will spend sufficient meaningful time with them to help each one be self-fulfilled and reach their maximum potential.

Display effective leadership skills. *When working with associates I will show them the right way by going first. By example I will inspire a following that is dedicated and voluntary. Together we will establish mutually defined goals and see that these goals are achieved.*

Go the second mile in serving others. *With each person I reach out to serve, I will humbly but confidently get inside their world with care, concern, and relevance to their needs. With sincerity I will lift them up to a higher sense of personal worth.*

The question is often asked: "How many unifying principles should a person have?" The number will vary for each individual and depends on a variety of factors. Ben Franklin had thirteen. You may have more or less. If you have too many, though, you may find your list somewhat cumbersome to manage.

We recommend that you start out by writing paragraphs of clarification for integrity, faith, love, and humility. Refer back to chapters 3-6 for help in defining these principles. Then add six to eight other unifying principles of your own to the list. More can always be added later as you continue building your superstructure.

Identifying and formulating your unifying principles into a cogent, understandable format is an important exercise that has the power to change your life forever.

Step 5: Prioritize your unifying principles.

Prioritizing is a process of valuing anticipated events you seek to control. We suggest a procedure of placing your most valued unifying principle at the top of the list, followed by the second most valued below it, and so forth. In order of importance, each unifying principle is preceded with an **AA** designation. For example:

AA1___ Love my family.

The next most highly valued unifying principle is designated with **AA2,** such as,

AA2___ Exercise super faith.

This procedure is followed until the complete list of unifying principles has been placed in numbered order of priority or importance.

To help you prioritize, ask yourself the following questions:

- *Which principles immediately come to mind as being the most significant?*

- *Which principles will yield the highest payoff to my self-esteem and productivity?*
- *Which principles will yield the quickest short-term results? Which will yield the greatest long-term results?*
- *Which principles will bring the most benefit to others, including my family and friends and my associates, and others in general?*
- *Which principles will result in the greatest detriment or suffering to me or to others if I do not align my behavior with them?*

Every unifying principle should be preceded with the **AA** symbol followed by its ranked number. This prioritizing mechanism will be covered in greater detail in the next chapter where the Unified Power System of goal planning and achievement will be discussed.

Be sure to place your unifying principles in a highly visible and accessible resource, such as a date book organizer, PDA, or laptop computer. This is called your Accessibility Center and should be whatever you use as a primary organizing tool to store and retrieve important information. This tool must be within your reach day and night, 168 hours a week.

Step 6: Evaluate your past and recent performance with each unifying principle.

Once your unifying principles are written, refined, and prioritized, the next step is to make a personal assessment of where your performance currently stands in relation to each of them.

For example, if one of your unifying principles is to demonstrate impeccable personal integrity by always being honest with yourself and others, you might ask yourself, "Over the past few weeks, have I been completely truthful in all my words and actions with family, friends, and associates?

The idea of looking back at your recent performance is to put yourself in touch with the reality of who you are right now, without rationalization or fear of outside recrimination. Your attention on what to change should focus on those unifying principles where your performance and values are currently not aligned, particularly on those principles you have designated to be among your highest priorities, such as your AA1, AA2, AA3, and so forth.

One woman described the process of writing and prioritizing her unifying principles as liberating and fulfilling. As she began to write, her values spilled right out on to the paper. She said, "I had my principles written in just a few days, and as I undertook this self-evaluation I found my behavior was congruent with almost every one of them. This strengthened confidence in myself in ways I had never before experienced."

Step 7: Bring your performance in line with your unifying principles.

Unified Power is a process. You must work at this process consistently and persistently every day for the rest of your life in order to achieve congruence between your performance and the principles you value most.

You may never be able to live every one of your unifying principles perfectly day in and day out, but there is inevitable improvement in incremental effort, as was demonstrated with Bert in chapter 2. Do not grow discouraged by small failures or by thinking the task ahead of you is too big. Once you make the commitment to never allow an exception to occur, with the help of daily visualization, planning and practice, you will find greater success in achieving your lofty aspirations.

When you correctly identify and apply your most valued unifying principles that are based on truths that have stood the test of time, your confidence and ability to control events you previously thought you could not control will grow exponentially. Trust yourself. Trust the process. Burn all bridges behind you. And do it now!

Unified Power Within Organizations

As it builds on truths that have stood the test of time, Unified Power is as applicable to organizations as it is to individuals. The process of its implementation within an organization is a challenging but worthwhile venture. And we would argue a necessary one. When optimally applied, every day can be a day of celebration for achievement and performance as integrated groups become strengthened with an increased sense of worth through congruous behavior and continuous improvement.

To better appreciate how Unified Power can work within organizations of any kind or size, let's now explore the unifying principles of three superstructure organizations that over time have excelled and endured well.

In the earliest days of IBM, its founder, T. J. Watson set forth the following three principles that he sought to engrain in the minds of every employee through continuous training at all levels.

1. Respect the individual.
2. Give quality customer service.
3. Commit to excellence.

Yet another organizational superstructure, Hewlett Packard, was founded in 1939 by Bill Hewlett and Dave Packard.

One of the first things Bill and Dave did in starting their company was to identify principles that would give vision and direction to employees. They called the following list the "HP Way."

1. Believe in people. We want all of our employees believing in each other and in our customers.
2. Grow in self-esteem. We believe that a person with high self-esteem will be a high producer.
3. Promote a sense of achievement.
4. Help each other.
5. Have open communication.
6. Reserve the right to make mistakes.
7. Promote training and education.
8. Provide security in employment.
9. Properly insure.
10. Manage with goals.

Jim Collins wrote, "The HP Way, as it became known, reflected a deeply held set of core values that distinguished the company more than any of its products." (Jim Collins, *Good to Great* [New York: HarperCollins, 2001], p. 193.)

The HP Way was made directly, continually, and meaningfully accessible to all workers, from senior management to the assembly line. Hewlett Packard's track record over many decades demonstrates how these principles have engendered both quality and productivity.

The final example of an organizational superstructure is found in the Hospital for Sick Children in Washington, D. C. Charles gives the following account of an experience he had with this remarkable organization.

One day the Chief Administrator of the Hospital for sick children, Constance Battle, asked me if I would be willing to teach our Time Power Seminar to her staff.

She explained that the ages of the children served by the hospital ranged from three into the teens. Every one of the children had the worst of physical deformities and maladies. Each child needed constant care. The hospital employed one nurse for every two children.

Before the seminar Dr. Battle took me on a tour of the hospital. At the main entrance was a list of profound guidelines that every employee embraced. They included:

- *Love the children.*
- *Humble yourself as a little child.*
- *With faith instill in each child hope and joy.*

Going from room to room I was amazed. The caretakers were all living the hospital's unifying principles in remarkable ways. I saw a lot of eye-to-contact, hugging, and children smiling and giggling. I was told that hospital employees not assigned to direct care positions, including office staff and custodians, would often on their own time and volition would spend time with the children.

At the end of the tour Dr. Battle told me that when she became the administrator two years earlier, the mortality rate was unusually high. So with her staff the above mentioned unifying principles were formulated and diligently implemented. From that point forward, the mortality rate of the children had considerably declined.

The Hospital for Sick Children had become a model and a wellness center of Unified Power, indeed an organizational superstructure.

T. J. Watson, Bill Hewlett, Dave Packer, and Constance Battle have provided examples on how to optimize quality productivity (see Company Unification model, next page) through clearly defined truths that lift up, strengthen, and unify. They exemplified true leadership in showing the right way by going first. They inspired a following. The following was voluntary. They established mutually defined goals based on guiding principles, and saw to it that these were practiced, not just preached. Each of these great leaders transformed their companies into superstructures.

Company Unification

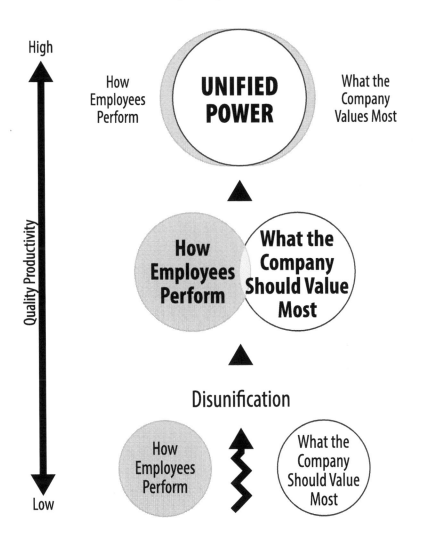

"*Organizations have to have values. But so do people. To be effective in an organization one's values must be completely compatible with the organization's values. Values are and should be the ultimate test.*" (*Peter F. Drucker*, The Essential Drucker, *p. 223.*)

Unified Power Steps

1. Prepare a list of what you value most in life. Make sure your unifying principles represent the ideal or highest forms of truth (like the four Unified Power Principles), and that they are mutually compatible.

2. Write each unifying principle as an action statement.

3. Write a paragraph of clarification under each unifying principle.

4. Prioritize your unifying principles in order of most important at the top, and then work your way down.

5. Evaluate your past/recent performance with each unifying principle, and be completely honest in your self-assessment.

6. Plan and visualize yourself living your unifying principles. Never allow an exception to occur.

7. Identify your Accessibility Center and use it every day to plan and measure performance with your unifying principles.

8. Follow the above steps for your organization, department or team. Educate and train continuously.

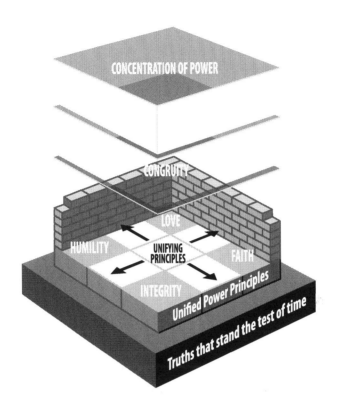

CHAPTER 11

Personal and Organizational Goals: **Empowering Your Superstructure**

"Goals are the building blocks of superstructure attainment, but only when they are secured upon a solid rock foundation of truths that have stood the test of time."

— *Charles R. Hobbs*

Not long ago an acquaintance emphatically declared to Charles, "I don't believe in goals!" Charles responded, "A goal is simply an idea directed toward a desired result. If you don't believe in goals, you must be dead."

All people, whether they realize it or not, have goals. If a goal is an anticipated event you seek to control with the expectation of a desired result, then even the acts of getting out of bed, driving to work, or mowing the lawn can be considered as goals, habitual as they may be.

As for goals that require more thought to be acted upon, there is a remarkable difference between passive planning that produces minimal activity and active, and high-value goals that generate optimal results through carefully planned and orchestrated activity.

Recently, a study found that only 3 percent of the population systematically writes goals, and that this same 3 percent excels in achieving remarkable results. Similarly, a study conducted at Wesleyan University and the University of California found that a person with high self-esteem performs at a higher level than those with low self-esteem. The study also found that people with high self-esteem consistently write and commit to goals. Contrast this to people with low self-esteem. They seldom engage in setting or completing goals of any kind. Clearly, there is a direct relationship between setting meaningful goals and achieving optimal performance.

In setting forth the following process for identifying and acting upon your goals, we recognize that some are naturally inclined to think in terms of goals while others choose to describe what they do in different terms. We also realize that the process can be adapted to suit individual preferences. What we strongly encourage, however, is that you extract from what we share those guidelines that will help *you* systematically build your own personal superstructure, and then follow through with daily planning in taking those steps that will release its full potential in your life.

The Great Pyramid near Cairo, Egypt was erected in the 2600s B.C. It is the largest of the Egyptian pyramids. Through the ages it has been spoken of as one of the "seven wonders of the world." It is certainly an enduring superstructure that has stood the test of time. In this chapter we will use it as a representation of the **Unified Power**

Pyramid of Quality Productivity (see model, page 124) for you to use in planning and achieving both your personal and work-related goals.

As with your personal superstructure, the great Egyptian pyramid has four corners at its foundation. In Unified Power terms, each of the cornerstones would symbolize integrity, faith, love, and humility. And, as we have already identified, there are other unifying power principles that, when added to the rest of your foundation, comprise your own self-styled superstructure.

Unifying principles are anticipated events we seek to control, which, by definition, are also goals. They are, however, broader generalizations on which your personal and company goals find their footing.

Once you have formulated your rock-solid foundation of unifying principles, it is time to add building blocks that will make up your own **Pyramid of Quality Productivity**. These building blocks consist of a selective formulation of anticipated events you seek to control that come together through a method of identifying and prioritizing long-range personal, or professional, goals from which you create more specific intermediate and immediate goals. We refer to this process as **Goal Continuity**.

When your unifying principles are clearly defined, refined, and prioritized, ask yourself: "What specifically do I (we) want to achieve?" This question triggers the development of long-range goals.

In writing your long-range goals, it will help to identify categories for balanced goal planning, such as:

- Family
- Intellectual
- Physical
- Financial
- Professional

When you have decided on your categories, write at least one or two long-range goals under each category. Keep in mind that long-range goals are typically further into the future. Some of these goals may take a year or two to achieve, while others may require a lifetime to accomplish.

Here are a few examples:

Family

_____ I will set aside meaningful time with my spouse and children to help each of them optimize their potential in life beginning (write starting date).

Intellectual

_____ I will read the biographies of great achievers beginning (write starting date).

Physical

_____ I will maintain excellent health through exercise and a healthy diet beginning (write starting date).

Financial

_____ I will pay myself first by saving or wisely investing a portion of every dollar I earn beginning (write starting date).

Professional

_____ I will get promoted/start my own company by (write date).

Next, prioritize these long-range goals by asking yourself the following questions:

- *Of all the goals I have written down, which is most supportive of my AA unifying principles?*

- *Which goals will yield the highest payoff?*
- *Which goals will be most useful to my family, my company, and myself in bringing about desired results in the next one to two years?*
- *What would happen if I do not achieve these goals? How much difficulty might I create for myself if I do not accomplish them?*
- *Would my failure to achieve any of these goals threaten the survival, general well being, or happiness of others?*

Early in his career, Charles adapted the standard symbols of **A, B, C,** and **D** for prioritizing unifying principles and goals as the simplest to implement. Let's take a closer look at how these symbols work best.

Remember: **AA** denotes truths that have stood the test of time (your unifying principles). Your most valued unifying principle is, therefore, marked with **AA1**. The next highest value receives an **AA2**, and so forth. (Refer to chapter 10 for how to prioritize your unifying principles.)

Long-range goals receive the designations of **A, B,** and **C**.

A denotes **Vital**. Webster's Dictionary defines vital as "life sustaining." You might also wisely add, "job sustaining," "marriage sustaining," and so on.

B denotes **Important**. These are still priority goals but are not as significant as the **A**s. However, they are still significant enough to not be far down on your list of goals.

C denotes **Some Value**. **C** priority goals are even less important than **B**s, and may or may not be important enough to accomplish, depending on the outcome of your **A** and **B** goals. Use your best judgment when deciding to commit to action on these types of goals.

D denotes **Waste of Time**, such as unproductive interruptions, preoccupation with irrelevant issues, or time spent tinkering with trivialities.

DD denotes **Dysfunction**. It identifies incongruous (or disunified) behaviors such as deception, failure to keep commitments, taking undeserved credit, dishonesty, making false judgments, arrogance, anger, fear, doubt, lying, or insubordination.

Ds and **DD**s are not goals, but rather symbols used for identifying incongruities. Every so often you should perform a self-evaluation or reality check to assess how you are spending your time. This can be done in a given day by making notations every fifteen minutes of where your time and attention was engaged. At the end of the day, assign one of the following priority symbols to each recorded event: **A, B, C, D,** or **DD**. Now compute the percentage of time you spent on each and evaluate how productive your day was.

To some extent, every one of us gets caught up in what are called "activity traps" by responding to low-priority urgencies. The hundreds of time logs we have run on people over the years have validated the Pareto Principle, which states: "20 percent of the value is in 80 percent of the time spent."

Once your long-range goals are defined, refined, and prioritized, write each one at the top of a separate sheet of paper. With each long-range goal ask yourself, "What actions do I need to take to achieve this goal?" These will become your intermediate goals.

Now make a list under each long-range goal of what needs to be done. Let's take "Maintain excellent health" as an example, with the assumption that you have prioritized it as your **A3** goal. Your page might look something like this:

A3___ I will maintain excellent health through exercise and a healthy diet.

___ Run three miles five days a week on the treadmill.

___ Lose twenty pounds by (write date).

___ Eliminate high calorie foods from all meals by (write date).

These intermediate goals are formulated from the long-range goal of "Maintain excellent health." You will now need to prioritize these goals using the same questions for prioritizing long-range goals. However, with each intermediate goal, use the lower case letters of **a, b,** or **c** to avoid confusion with your long-range goals.

After your long-range and intermediate goals have been prioritized, place them with your list of unifying principles where they will be most directly and meaningfully accessible, such as in your Accessibility Center. These goals need to be continuously at your fingertips so you can draw upon them in your daily planning and throughout the day.

Each day during your early morning solitude planning, you will draw from your long-range, or intermediate goals, and write **immediate goals** to accomplish that day. Your list of immediate goals then becomes your **Daily Action List**, which you will prioritize as lowercase **aa**, **bb**, **cc**, and so forth.

There are three basic steps to follow when preparing a Daily Action List.

Step 1: Review your unifying principles and decide which one is the most important to work on that day.

Let's say you select your **AA1** unifying principle of "Have personal integrity." At this point you need to apply the principle of goal continuity by asking yourself, "What specific action of integrity should I focus on today?"

To answer this question you will need to define an action that is not only specific enough to be attainable, but also measurable. So you might write as the first immediate goal in your Daily Action List:

aa1___ Today I will honor every commitment I have made to everyone with whom I associate, including being on time to every meeting, returning phone calls, and completing every assignment.

Notice the **aa1** designation is in lower case letters. This means that this immediate goal, based on your **AA1** unifying principle of "Have personal integrity," is your most vital priority to accomplish that day. The underscore line is where you will place a checkmark at the end of the day as you pat yourself on the back for being victorious.

Every Daily Action List should have an **aa1** ___ at the top written in specific, measurable terms based on at least one of your unifying principles. Be sure to keep every immediate goal you write specific enough that it can be accomplished in a relatively short period of time. For example, don't write, "Do QZ report," if doing so is going to take you two days. Instead, break the project into steps and write, "Complete QZ report outline by 3 P.M. this afternoon."

Step 2: Prioritize your list by asking the following questions:

1. *Of all my long-range and intermediate high priority goals, which should I work on today?*
2. *What projects will give the highest return for the time invested today?*
3. *What projects will be the greatest threat to my success or that of my company if I don't accomplish them today?*
4. *What projects does my boss consider most vital for me to accomplish today?*

5. *Which goals on my previous Daily Action Lists do I absolutely need to get done today?*

We have just gone through the Unified Power process of Goal Continuity. Notice in the Unified Power Pyramid of Quality Productivity the progression of goals.

The Pyramid of Quality Productivity

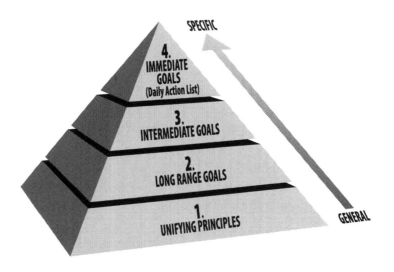

Step 3: Visualize achieving your goals through the process of anticipatory planning. Take at least five minutes after prioritizing your Daily Action List to visualize yourself going through the necessary steps to accomplish each goal.

Years ago Charles attended an exhibit of the accomplished sculptor, Florence Hansen. After her impressive presentation to a group of admirers, she was asked to share what she did to create such inspiring works of art. What she shared offers a useful blueprint for how setting goals and visualizing accomplishing them work together to produce optimal results.

Florence said:

Before I start a project I do an incredible amount of research in order to understand the attributes or personality of the subject. I then visualize in my mind exactly what the finished product will look like when it is finished.

Then I create the entire image with clay, shaping and reshaping with material that is much easier to work with than marble. After I complete this model, I search until I find a block of marble without blemish that meets my exact specifications.

Then with my tools I chip away at the marble, one piece at a time, one section at a time, day after day, until I have finished.

The Urgent, the Vital, and the Trivial

No discussion on prioritizing would be complete without bringing up productivity's best friend and worst enemy: **URGENT!**

Charles E. Hummel said:

The [vital] task rarely must be done today, or even this week. The urgent task calls for instant action. The momentary appeal of these tasks seems irresistible and they devour our energy. But in the light of time's perspective their deceptive prominence fades. With a sense of loss we recall the vital task we pushed aside. We realize we've become slaves to the tyranny of the urgent.

Urgent is a stimulus that always elicits immediate response. During the past week how many interruptions did you encounter that on the surface appeared to be urgent but then ended up being trivial? What did you really accomplish in addressing all of these urgencies? If you were to keep a log of every time someone dumped urgency in your lap—a child, spouse, boss, or associate—you would be shocked by how many times this happens, and how these "urgencies" take you away from more important, vital priorities.

Granted, urgency does generate a certain level of productivity through immediate action. With each urgency comes a sudden surge of mental or physical energy. Often, an increase in activity will result, but we must not confuse activity with productivity, especially in terms of controlling events and accomplishing high value goals.

Take, for example, the proverbial "busybody." These people are experts in the urgent, and rarely contribute worthwhile results because they remain steadfastly engaged in the trivial. They expend considerable energy in a flurry of activities on things that matter least, and in actions that don't amount to any meaningful results.

Imagine you are working on a vital, time-critical project and the telephone rings. You don't recognize the number on your caller ID, but what do you do? You answer the call. Now imagine it's the wrong number, or, worse yet, it's somebody trying to sell you something. This happens all the time and is a classic example of a **D** incongruity at work. Why did you answer? For the simple reason that we've been conditioned to think a ringing telephone is urgent.

Let's look at urgent in a different way. You are approaching a busy intersection at forty miles per hour when the light turns yellow. Is this a stimulus that elicits a response? Yes. Does the yellow light, soon to be red, call for immediate action? Yes. In this case, it is both urgent and vital that you make a decision and act on it immediately.

What most people are prone to do is confuse the urgent with the vital. The tendency in most cases is to deal with urgency as though it were vital, when in actuality it is not. A yellow light turning red in a busy intersection, of course, is both vital and urgent. A phone ringing from an unrecognized number during the middle of doing something really important is not.

On its own, "urgent" seldom relates to priorities and highly valued goals, yet it often has such a huge influence on how we act. We almost always yield to urgent stimuli, especially when the source is a spouse or boss.

Imagine your wife giving you an important "honey do" project that has to be finished before the in-laws visit in two weeks. She clearly defines your **A** priorities for you, and you agree to them.

Now, what would most guys do in this situation? What would you do? Likely, you would go back to your own agenda, tinkering on your own projects, playing golf with your buddies, and basically procrastinating. After all, there is no call for immediate action since the in-laws won't be arriving for another two weeks. Nothing is pressing. There is no urgency, right? But what happens three days before they arrive? All of your other **A** priority goals get pushed aside to accomplish the urgent ones in front of you. This is not quality productivity. It is self-preservation.

Back in Charles' university days, he had a close friend named Ernie who was not like the rest of his classmates. He would always sit on the front row close to the professor where there was less distraction. Charles remembers sitting next to Ernie, hoping that some of his intelligence might transfer to him through osmosis.

On the first day of class, the professor distributed a handout setting forth his expectations. On the paper was a list of books to read. The professor made it clear that the final grade would be based solely on one final exam. Every student would be expected to answer questions from both the listed books and from the professor's lectures.

You can guess what happened the night before the final exam. Charles and his other buddies spent the night cramming in a crowded library. What do you think happened the next day? Ernie received the highest score on the final exam.

Are you ready now for *your* big exam? Below is a grid with four boxes. There are only two possible answers per box: **Gets Done** or **Doesn't Get Done.** Take a few minutes to think through each box before you place your answer in each box.

	Vital	Not Vital
Urgent		
Not Urgent		

Let's now take a look at your answers. What is the consequence if you face an event that is both Vital and Urgent as in the upper left box? It **Gets Done**, right? But, is it the vital or the urgent that ensures it gets done? Remember, it is usually the urgent that moves us to immediate action. For much of the time people have vital events they are not doing because these events are not considered urgent.

What did you put in the upper right box for Not Vital and Urgent? If you answered, **Gets Done,** you are correct. What makes it get done? Again, the urgency. What if it is Vital and Not Urgent? Does it get done? More often than not, it **Doesn't Get Done,** even though it is vital.

The same thing is true for Not Vital and Not Urgent; it **Doesn't Get Done**, unless you happen to be one of those unproductive busybodies mentioned earlier.

Now, just for fun, make a quick personal assessment of how you spend your time on any given day. How many hours of the day do you think you spend on vital events versus trivial (or urgent) events? "Vital" means work that has a high payoff where activity will result in quality productivity. "Trivial" means limited value of importance but lots of activity. In a typical waking day, if you were to spend one or two hours on "vital" events and the rest on "trivial," you would probably be like most average people.

Charles once worked with an electronics company in Colorado. There was a senior manager who was highly respected in a division of 2,500 people. At a follow-up meeting with Charles, the manager said, "Charles, I didn't do exactly what you advised in performance planning. I decided I would do exactly what I've always done except I ran a time log for five days to see what my vital versus trivial ratio was."

He went on to explain that his personal assessment resulted in a one to nine ratio for a typical working day: one hour on the vital and nine hours on the trivial. He was constantly putting out fires more than he was producing actual results. What do you think that did to his self-esteem and quality productivity?

Charles asked him what he did about it. The manager said, "I spent two solid days developing my unifying principles, high priority goals, and other guidelines you taught us to implement. The next week I ran another time log to see how I stacked up. The results were phenomenal. My allocations of time completely flipped. I spent almost nine hours on the vital and one on the trivial."

Not every person will experience such dramatic results, but more people fall under the category of the "Trivial Many" than the "Vital Few."

Goals with Your Organization

The Unified Power process for writing workplace goals is basically the same as with personal goals, except for a few modifications:

1. The categories for company-balanced goal planning with unifying principles and long-range goals will, of course, be different than for personal life goals, and will vary depending on the company and the job. By way of example, categories might include the following:

- Budget and Finance
- Sales and Marketing
- Product Development
- Human Resources and Training

2. To maximize quality productivity within an organization, every employee's goals should be firmly aligned with the company's strategic plan.

3. Every employee must consistently be held accountable by his or her direct report in goal planning and achievement.

4. As with personal life goals, the company's unifying goals and principles should be congruent with an employee's personal unifying principles.

5. In addition to a personal prioritized Daily Action List, a company-prioritized Daily Action List should be developed.

Guidelines for Transforming Your Organization Into a Superstructure

In chapter 10 we explored three enduring superstructure organizations (IBM, Hewlett Packard, and the Hospital for Sick Children) that empowered themselves with pervasive communications and training procedures to indoctrinate every employee in their respective organization with simple but powerful unifying principles.

Here is another thought from IBM's T. J. Watson.

I firmly believe that any organization, in order to survive and achieve success, must have a sound set of beliefs on which it premises all its policies and actions. Next, I believe that the most important single factor in corporate success is faithful adherence to these beliefs, and finally, I believe if an organization is to meet the challenge of a changing world, it must be prepared to change everything about itself except those beliefs as it moves through corporate life. (A Business and Its Beliefs.)

As with a personal superstructure, it is essential that an organization's superstructure be built upon a rock-solid foundation of truths that have stood the test of time. The four cornerstones of integrity, faith, love, and humility are as applicable to organizations as they are to individuals.

What, then, can be done to make team members values compatible with those of the company? The answer is for the organization and its employees to share and embrace the four Unified Power Principles as part of their superstructure's foundation.

The process of inculcation starts with senior management using *Unified Power* as a primary guide in preparing the strategy for implementation of the Unified Power System in the organization. Keep in mind that the organization's unifying principles, as vital as they are, represent only the foundation of the superstructure.

When the foundation is in place, building blocks of anticipated events are added to form the walls of the superstructure. These building blocks are the company's goals, which, of course, are identified and put into action by senior management. In other words, the organization's strategic plan should consist of prioritized goals built upon the foundation of the four Unified Power Principles.

When the strategic plan is in place, and when senior management is committed to implementing the Unified Power System, the plan should then be communicated to the leaders of divisions, departments, and teams so that every employee is trained—all the way from CEO to the janitor. Each manager should have in hand that portion of the strategic plan that, when carried out, will meet all expectations of senior management in strengthening the company superstructure. Every team member should be committed to a position description that outlines and aligns his or her prioritized expectations.

Unified Power Steps

1. Now that your Unifying Principles are written, refined, and prioritized, you are ready to construct the Unified Power Pyramid of Quality Productivity by engaging in the following goal continuity steps:

  a. Say to yourself, "In addition to my unifying principles, what else do I want out of life? This will lead you to write one or two long-range personal life goals under each of the categories of family, intellectual, physical, financial, and professional.

  b. Prioritize these goals.

  c. Now, with each long-range goal, ask yourself, "What actions do I need to take to achieve this goal?" Answering this question will lead to your writing smaller, more specific intermediate goals.

  d. Prioritize your intermediate goals.

  e. Organize and place your prioritized long-range and intermediate goals, along with your unifying principles, where they will be directly, continuously, and meaningfully accessible for your daily planning.

2. Select your own Accessibility Center, which you should have with you wherever you go. It could be a printed organizer, such as a Day-Timer, or an electronic device.

3. In your early morning solitude planning time, prioritize a Daily Action List of immediate goals to act upon that day. Always include at least one unifying principle goal at the top of the list.

4. Using the Unified Power system of goal continuity, write, refine, and prioritize your long-range and intermediate goals within the company. Every workday, prepare and act upon a prioritized Daily Action List for your specific job.

5. Take control of the tyranny of the urgent in your life by avoiding the **Ds** and some of the **Cs**, and obliterating the **DDs**. Place a strong sense of urgency on the high **As** and the higher-ranked **Bs**.

6. Visualize yourself (or team) accomplishing all high value goals each morning during a period of solitude or anticipatory planning.

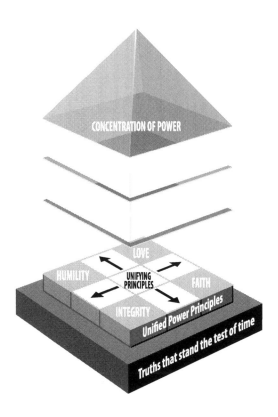

CHAPTER 12

Completing Your Superstructure

"We are born with faculties and powers capable of almost anything, such as at least would carry us further than can be easily imagined; but it is only the exercise of those powers which gives us ability and skill in anything, and leads us towards perfection."

—John Locke

There is a level of complexity inherent in building anything that has lasting value. And yet there is a remarkable simplicity as well, if we follow the Unified Power blueprint, which will guide the construction of our own personal or organizational superstructure. The question to consider now is, just where might the plan we've presented take you?

In the introduction to this book, we introduced you to a friend Charles once made by the name of Martha. You may recall that when Charles first met her she was a departmental secretary with a rather lofty ambition—to be the president of the company she worked for within three years. To provide a real-life and appropriate conclusion to all the parts and processes we have shared relative to building a personal superstructure, here is the rest of Charles's experience:

Three years after I had visited with Martha about her long-range goal, I received a call from the new human resource director of the company in Detroit I had consulted with years earlier. He said, "We are calling to ask that you come back to our company for a one-day follow-up with the seminar participants you taught three years ago."

I was quite surprised and said, "With other companies, I have done a few follow-ups soon after the initial training, but I've never done one three years later.

He replied, "Well, think of it as a refresher course. Will you come?" I said, "Of course I will."

When I arrived at his office he said, "I would like to introduce you to the new president of our company. We walked into the president's office, and there at the desk was Martha. She stood up, shook my hand warmly, and said, "Welcome back, Charles."

This was the afternoon before our group follow-up session, and Martha and I had time to talk. I said, "Martha, I have not forgotten your A1 professional goal you shared with me three years ago when you were a secretary—that you would become president of the company. How did you do it?

She said, "I simply followed the guidelines you shared with us in writing productivity goals along with your other assignments."

As we visited, Martha shared what had transpired in her work environment over the previous three years. In the spirit of humility she expressed the love she felt for her associates and for the company. She then explained that upon becoming a department head, she introduced the Pyramid of Quality Productivity to those who reported to her, which she said helped them define and achieve their unifying principles and goals as they fulfilled their portion of the company's strategic plan.

I learned that throughout the three years she had followed an early morning solitude planning period every day where she visualized aligning her performance with her unifying principles, formulated her personal and company priorities into a Daily Action List drawing upon her long-range and intermediate goals, and applied the principle of accessibility, which is:

"In order to accomplish a goal, become proficient with a skill, or take command of a body of knowledge, make that goal, skill, or body of knowledge directly, continually, and meaningfully accessible to yourself."

The next day I had the opportunity to visit with some of Martha's subordinates, who shared comments such as:

- *"When Martha makes a commitment, she always keeps it."*
- *"What you see is what you get. She is a person to be trusted, a person of integrity."*
- *"She is always there for me when I need her."*
- *"Her entrepreneurial skill is just what our company needs."*

As I was flying home after completing our follow-up session, I thought to myself, "Here is a self-unified woman of super faith with a remarkable concentration of power. What a pillar of strength Martha is to all who know her—and what a remarkable example she is of what we each have the potential to achieve."

For three years Martha had followed the necessary steps for building her superstructure with precision and determination—each and every day!

Such is the potential within each and every one of us. In our own way, by applying the Doctrine of Self-Unification and developing

Congruity, Competency Plus, and Concentration of Power, we can follow the example of Martha and grab hold of the stars. Depending upon our own level of faith, commitment, and determination, some of us may only reach the treetops. But even that is a much better view than hugging the ground in conformity with the crowd.

Each of us has the same opportunity—to build upon an immovable foundation based on truths that have stood the test of time, to identify unifying principles unique to our personalities and intentions, and to be absolutely committed and congruous in taking the daily steps that will build our personal and organizational superstructures.

The journey will not be without its challenges, and the focus and discipline required will sometimes stretch you beyond what appear to be your limits. But the outcomes will be just as exhilarating as those experienced by the astronauts who, after years of intensive effort, look down from heights that were once only a dream.

In building your superstructure, you will achieve levels of self-esteem and quality productivity you never thought possible for yourself or for your organization. Indeed, you will experience Unified Power.

Index

About the Authors

In 1970 Charles R. Hobbs received his doctorate in learning and teaching theory under some of the most brilliant minds in his field of study at Columbia University in New York City. It was there that he became convinced that lives could be changed, not for just a few days, weeks or months, but for a lifetime if people were given the right training and tools.

That germ of an idea ultimately took root and grew into the Time Power System, the very first time management training program of its kind. Charles and his associates taught the seminar throughout the United States and other countries which gave rise directly or indirectly to numerous other programs that were largely based on the internationally acclaimed principles Charles developed. In addition Charles wrote the best-selling book *Time Power*, which was named in 1993 as one of the top twenty time-tested business management books by the editors of Executive Book Summaries.

Unified Power could well be considered an easy-to-read graduate course of Time Power, for it expands in-depth on the preeminent Doctrine of Self-Unification that was first introduced in the Time Power Seminar and book.

Greg W. Allison is a 20-year brand and marketing veteran holding various management positions in the retail and service industry, as well as being a consultant and owning his own marketing services agency. He is currently Senior Director of Global Brands & Innovation at a large international franchise organization, and lives and works in Salt Lake City, Utah.

Greg's lessons learned and achievements earned over his career have helped shape his belief in the importance of principle-based leadership in delivering long-term value. The practice of developing strategic plans and key performance initiatives based on time-honored values, often absent in Corporate America, has long been a passion of Greg.

The collaboration with Charles on Unified Power is the culmination of Greg's experience that personal and professional values can, and must, co-exist in order to achieve lasting success and happiness in life and career. Greg laid the groundwork for the Unified Power superstructure model that, when put into everyday practice and application, can empower not only the individual but an entire organization in optimizing quality productivity in a thoughtful meaningful way.

Visit CharlesRHobbs.com for additional information.

Made in the USA
Charleston, SC
28 June 2013